P9-BZZ-797

The F

S. Y. A

The Fiction of
S. Y. AGNON

ʎ

by Baruch Hochman

Cornell University Press

ITHACA AND LONDON

Copyright © 1970 by Cornell University

All rights reserved. Except for brief quotations in a review, this book, or parts thereof, must not be reproduced in any form without permission in writing from the publisher. For information address Cornell University Press, 124 Roberts Place, Ithaca, New York 14850.

English translations from "Agunot," "Vehaya he'akov lemishor," "Agadat hasofer," "Hanidaḥ," "Bin'arenu uvizkenenu," *Sipur pashut,* *Temol shilshom,* and *Hakhnassat kala* were made by Baruch Hochman with the permission of Schocken Books Inc., publishers of the works of S. Y. Agnon. Copyright © 1970 by Schocken Books Inc.

A Guest for the Night, translated by Misha Louvish, copyright © 1968 by Schocken Books Inc., is quoted by permission of Schocken Books Inc. and Victor Gollancz, Ltd.

First published 1970

Standard Book Number 8014-0558-0
Library of Congress Catalog Card Number 74-106354

PRINTED IN THE UNITED STATES OF AMERICA
BY VAIL-BALLOU PRESS, INC.

For Simon Halkin
with gratitude

Contents

Preface

The Nobel Prize for Literature is an odd institution. Year in, year out, it is conferred on a writer. Sometimes we are delighted with the wisdom of the choice. Sometimes we are outraged at its folly. As often as not, we are startled to learn that its laureate exists. Time and again the award turns our attention to writers whose eminence—nay, whose existence—we have hardly imagined. Then the man and his work nudge their way into our consciousness, the man himself barely comprehensible, the work often hardly understandable in the terms of our familiar literary awareness.

Yet the writers in question are generally the lions of their literary worlds, men with a lifetime of work and honors behind them. For the most part, coming to their work, we sense that it is finely wrought and, in its own terms, somehow meaningful. But both its subtleties and its meaning tend to elude us, for they reflect unfamiliar traditions.

This is not merely a matter of blatantly exotic qualities. Very often, the large outlines of intention are comprehensible. What eludes us is the peculiar balance, in the work of an original artist, of idiosyncrasy and convention. Even in our own tradition, the great masters face this hazard; the alien gifted and sometimes minor writers turned up by the Nobel are even more vulnerable.

This, surely, was the case with S. Y. Agnon, the Israeli writer who shared the Nobel award with Nellie Sachs in 1966. Agnon is incontestably the dean of Hebrew novelists; he is probably the most admired writer in Israel. But very little of his work had appeared in English: a translation of *The Bridal Canopy*, his first major novel, was published in 1937, and intermittent works in the decades that followed, but there was nothing major until his *Two Tales* came out on the eve of his receiving the Nobel. Agnon was almost wholly unknown to the ordinary reader of English, and he was likely to remain so. The fine craftsmanship of his tales was evident to the discerning. When the translations were good, one sensed that something more was present. But that something was largely unidentifiable.

And the Nobel award did little to change this impression. The citation itself merely defined Agnon's place in the tradition of Jewish letters, and placed him—as it placed Nellie Sachs—in the context of the tragedy of European Jewry in our century. Nor did the image of the man, as conveyed through the news media after the Nobel award, illuminate the work. Indeed, what one saw of him seemed chiefly to reinforce the sense that he was odd, exotic, and elusive. To see Agnon on television was to watch a quaint old man who played funny, teasing games. Softly wrinkled, with a wry cast in his eye, Agnon would push his skull cap rakishly to the side and play the elderly gnome: a folksy octogenarian who bowed and scraped and directed pious ironies at himself and at the world.

The "facts" did not help much either. One learned that he is a Galician Jew whose mother tongue is Yiddish and whose culture is essentially Orthodox, but who writes in

Hebrew and who has spent the better part of his adult life in Israel. One learned that he practices the old rituals but is an accomplished modernist in prose. One heard that he has a deep affection for the old, Orthodox culture of Eastern Europe, that he is steeped in its texts, and that he presents its common folk in his stories. On the other hand, one heard that his work reflects the spiritual crises of the modern Jew, to a degree and with a subtlety unsurpassed in his tradition.

But none of this information was very helpful. Even to the reader with a modicum of knowledge and a variety of keys and cues, the best qualities of the work remained elusive. The folksy tales, with their roots in the East European Jewish village culture, somehow seemed stale and static, and the modernist tales often seemed unnecessarily obscure. The reasons were not only the intrinsic unfamiliarity of the material, but also Agnon's peculiarities, the ambiguities of his tales, and his relation to his tradition.

For, whatever he is writing about, the central facts about Agnon are the monumental ambivalence that animates his work and the deep contradictions that inform it. Again and again in his fiction, Agnon refuses to define the vision he affirms or to establish clearly the facts on which he will take his stand. Hence there is rarely a moment of authoritative statement, like those we recognize in the self-declaring masterpieces of literature—statement that makes both immediate and ultimate demands on our attention. Rather, we are tangled in an elegant tissue of consciousness that seems meant to be enjoyed for its tenuousness.

Yet there is much of substance and value in the fabric of Agnon's fiction, and much of that substance inheres in its ambiguities. It is not, to be sure, work of commanding mastery that Agnon produces. Indeed, it is fiction that often fails to turn on its own assumptions and that often indulges in a crippling fancifulness. At the same time, if it is regarded according to the standards it sets for itself, Agnon's fiction maintains the highest level of craftsmanship and has an unswerving fidelity to the range of experience it engages. It takes up, moreover, a wide span of issues, and projects them in ways that have ramifications beyond the confines of the parochial world it seems to render.

Anyone approaching Agnon must accept both the scope and the limits of his interests. The intention of the present study is to illuminate those interests and to define Agnon's treatment of them in his major works. I approach the body of the work through a pair of late parables that embrace its central themes, and briefly sketch the development of those themes, placing them in the context of Agnon's life and times. Then I examine the major fiction in more or less chronological order. Finally, I attempt briefly to assess the achievement, both in terms of the standards it sets for itself and of the standards that might be imposed by the canons of modern literature.

In doing so, I hope not only to open a way into the Agnon country for readers to whom it is wholly alien, but also to chart some of its obscure reaches for readers who have visited it before. Believing that the essential act of criticism is an act of judgment rather than of explication, I go beyond elucidation in attempting to evolve grounds for a critical assessment of Agnon's work, in its parts and as a whole.

ACKNOWLEDGMENTS

Marion Hoagland has taken a long-standing gadfly's interest in my interest in Agnon. Her skeptical attention has played its part in the generation of the notions that inform this study. So has her timely suggestion that I undertake the essay from which it grew. Allen Mandelbaum, too, has been more than kind in encouragement. I would like to thank Avigdor Arikha, who once threw out some remarks that proved seminal, and Gershon Shaked, who was magnanimous in his bibliographic attentions. Agnon's own hospitable conversation in Jerusalem during the summer of 1967, combined with his staunch refusal to talk shop, provided an ideal context for thinking about his work. For that, too, I am grateful.

Betty Dagan was prolific of moral and technical help. So were Ruth and Steven Frieder, Zeva and Don Shapiro, Maier Deshell, and my wife Barbara—all of whom read generously and did not stint judgment.

The better part of this essay was written under a grant from the National Foundation for the Humanities, which I wish to thank for leisure afforded.

I wish to thank Theodore Schocken and Schocken Books for generosity in making material from Agnon's work available for citation.

I am grateful as well to the editors of *Commentary* and *Judaism* for permission to reprint, in somewhat altered versions, the essay which became the first chapter of this study (from *Commentary*, by permission; copyright © by the American Jewish Committee) and the essay which became the second chapter (from *Judaism*, Spring, 1968).

The editors at Cornell University Press have been very helpful with the manuscript.

BARUCH HOCHMAN

Jerusalem
January 1970

The Fiction of
S. Y. AGNON

[1]
Agnon's Quest:
An Overview

[1]

S. Y. Agnon's most informed readers think of him as an epic writer, as the novelist par excellence in his tradition. His fiction spans five to six generations of Jewish life in East Central Europe and Palestine, from the Hasidic revival at the end of the eighteenth century through the Zionist revival at the end of the nineteenth, and beyond that into the present worlds of European and Israeli Jewry. Yet, these readers maintain, Agnon's fiction—for all its diversity of scene and action, and all its range of tone and texture—is as coherent as the Faulknerian epic of southern life and as rigorously ordered as the many-tiered novels of Balzac and Proust. And, they insist, the overall movement of spirit in Agnon's fictive world drives toward dilemmas that transcend the parochial issues of that world; his work, indeed, is said to project a vision of the human condition that is universally valid for our times.[1]

These are large claims, and, within limits, they seem to be borne out by the scope of Agnon's interests. At the same time, however, they disregard the unique qualities of his achievement and go against the grain of his essential gift. Agnon's powers are not primarily the powers of a novelist; he has no gusto, no thirst for experience, no substantial gift of empathy. He has never been concerned with the plastic creation of character, and he has, on the whole, shunned the task of fleshing out human responses within the finely meshed web of social relationships. His gift is essentially a lyric one, though his lyricism is coupled with a nearly misanthropic thrust of satiric imagination. The grand felicities of his prose, like those of Mann and Proust, of Kafka and Joyce, come to serve as a vehicle for meditation upon the life of the soul, for a meditation that appropriates the actualities of the outer world in order to evoke the sense of an elusive subjectivity.[2]

That subjectivity is ordinarily ill at ease within its immediate surroundings. Even in the relatively stable East European village culture, which Agnon is fond of portraying, feeling always strives to go beyond the tangible; it aspires toward a realm of communion with the deity or of union with the dead, with whom people sustain their vital bonds. In Agnon's modernist work, which reflects the turmoil of the twentieth-century world, feeling reaches beyond the tangible and, finding no stable point of contact with anything, churns about and lapses into incoherence.[3]

One of the most remarkable qualities of Agnon's work is the way it stays in touch with such essential modes of yearning subjectivity. Still more remarkable is the way it projects those modes into the various periods and milieus which interest him. Agnon so places the subjectivity in the context of historical reality that its origins and ends lie open to our scrutiny. At the same time, we have the sense that Agnon's involvement with this haunting inwardness is what sets a final limit to his achievement as a writer. All too often, his entire effort is to evoke and protect it; all too often, he does not move beyond its enchanted aura to a confrontation with all the realities, subjective and objective, that bear upon it. Still, he manages to exploit it in a way that fitfully illuminates his life and his times.

[2]

The essential qualities of Agnon's work are epitomized in two late tales that have been paired in their English translation, and that probably constitute the best introduction to his work. "Betrothed" (1943) and "Ido and Enam" (1950) are among Agnon's most accomplished fiction, dealing with characteristic motifs in characteristic ways.[4] Beyond that, they have the uncommon virtue of reflecting directly upon his entire imaginative enterprise. "Ido and Enam," especially, establishes a framework for considering the interests and attitudes that animate so much of Agnon's fiction.

The two tales have strong narrative and thematic affinities. Both of them reflect an obsession with the past—the one with a personal past, the other with a communal one—and both treat that obsession with clinical detachment. Both inhabit a night world dominated by moon-struck women. Both deal with the experience of scholars engrossed in esoteric disciplines, the one with a marine biologist, the other with an ethnologist. In both, the action hinges on a rejection of Eros. And both are ultimately concerned with the folly of commitment to rational disciplines in the face of deep irrational desires which hark back to the archaic experience of the individual or the race.

Susan, the heroine of "Betrothed," appears in Jaffa to remind Jacob Rechnitz of the vows of eternal fidelity they had taken in their childhood. Extremely passive, Jacob cannot act on his vow; he drifts in an ambience of a dead factuality. At the end, when six maidens of his acquaintance race along a strip of pounding surf for a crown of seaweed from his collection—we never know whether this is actually happening or whether he is dreaming it all—Susan appears from nowhere, in her nightdress, and wins the race, the crown, and, presumably, Jacob's hand. As they run, Jacob, like one entranced, sees Susan as his mother kneeling at his side and fixing his tie; she is identified for him with the moon, the sea, the tides—with the great, agitated mother of all being, all desire. To this identification and all it implies, he has been able to relate only by an act of intellectual distancing. Rechnitz studies the sea and its spawn scientifically, in a way that cuts him off from the feminine lure of life itself, which has grown deathly in his imagination through identification with the maternal presence.

There is in "Betrothed" a peculiar mingling of real and dreamlike states, of Jacob's drab everyday existence in sleepy Jaffa before World War I and the fairy-tale romance of his inner life. Susan is a real girl from Vienna, but she is also a figment of Jacob's inner being. There is terror, for us and for him, in her charmed night apparition, but there is also wonder and the exhilaration of release. As the seventh maiden in Jacob's constellation, she is the Sabbath Queen and she is—or rather becomes—*Shoshanat Yaakov*, the "rose of Jacob" in the Purim song, and as such she suggests the gaiety of the Purim feast. In the final fulfillment, she bursts the spirit's sleep; death becomes life, the principle of terror the principle of love and reconciliation. At the end, without psychologizing, we have a sense of the resolution of a significant spiritual process, obscure but luminous, and touched with awe.[5]

A similar sense of spiritual process dominates "Ido and Enam," which is also concerned with the resurrection of a lost past—this time from a more highly universalized point of view. Gemulah, the Susan of this tale, is the last repository of the traditions of a warrior tribe that has preserved the heroic ways of ancient Israel in the timeless mountains of central Asia. Gamzu, a one-eyed dealer in rare books and manuscripts, has found her and carried her off as his wife to modern Jerusalem. But it is Ginat she loves, a handsome ethnologist who has recorded as they came from her lips the marvelous hymns of ancient Enam and the grammar of the lost tongue of Ido.

Removed from her native place, she has taken to her bed, a chronic invalid who torments her husband, rising only to sleepwalk at the full of the moon. Only magical charms that look, says the narrator (referring back to "Betrothed"), "like the seaweed fished from the sea by Rechnitz at Jaffa," can prevent her nightwalking. But Gamzu lost the charms when he sold the book in which they had been placed. The book has been bought by Ginat, whom Gemulah seeks out, in her nocturnal wanderings, to sing him the song of Grofit, which can be sung only once in a lifetime and which consumes both the singer and him to whom she sings. Ginat will not listen to her song, but one night when she walks on a roof in a trance, singing the song, she carries him to his death as he tries to save her from a fall. Since she and Ginat have died, the haunting

beauty that she embodies and he has transcribed can now
be glimpsed only in Ginat's books, out of which it "shines,
like a light, glimmering."

Susan, linked to the sea and the tides, suggests a lost
world of infinite desire, rooted in the personal past of a single individual. Gemulah, linked to the moon and the stars,
suggests a generic past, rooted in the history of the race.
The archaic world from which she comes belongs to a time
before recorded history; it exists in a sort of golden age in
which all things hang together, in which the center cannot
but hold—an idyllic world where natural, tribal, and political harmony prevails, and where the religious and the
erotic are one. Her name itself is suggestive, meaning "the
weaned one," "the reciprocal one," or "reward"; a derivative of the same name, Gumlidata, meaning something like
"reciprocult," is used in another Agnon parable, "Forevermore."

Gamzu, whose name means "this too" but also suggests
an Aramaic term for grafting in fig culture, is the man who
tries to patch things up—to make sense, in other words, of
the forms of Orthodoxy in which he cannot altogether believe. In attempting to domesticate the recalcitrant girl, he
dooms himself to suffering, sterility, and bereavement. For
Gemulah, in name the reciprocal, or the reciprocated one,
cannot reciprocate his kind of desire, while Ginat—even
though his name suggests a truncated form of the phrase
describing the garden of love in the Song of Songs—cannot
reciprocate hers. He can, however, with the monstrous detachment of his "scientific" pursuit, penetrate the mysteries
of the being she embodies, and yet this penetration exposes
him, willy-nilly, to her fatal song.

The very scene of the action in "Ido and Enam" fixes its frame of reference. Agnon in his fiction plays continually with the redemptive, messianic associations of Jerusalem, the Holy City, which signifies security and integrity, as opposed to the Diaspora (the Exile), where rootlessness and insecurity prevail. Yet the city of Jerusalem is also of this world, is a modern environment of alienation, disruption, and fragmentation. Even his earliest, most lyric tale, "Agunot," projects a sense of the tragic chanciness of the best of possible arrangements in the best of possible towns. As if to emphasize this sense of necessary contingency, he has the names of most of the characters in "Ido and Enam" —who are in fact homeless—begin with the letter *G*, which could stand for the Hebrew words for either redemption or exile, or both (*geulah* and *golah*); the story thus succeeds in suggesting that what the seeker of redemption finds is only another form of spiritual and sexual exile. But Agnon, at the last, will not relinquish the possiblity of achieving at least a vision of redemption. The light of the spirit that shines out of the works of Ginat affirms once again the possibility of realizing in the flesh, and in history, the values of beauty and truth.[6]

"Ido and Enam" is a powerful and complex tale. I happened to read it in Jerusalem when it first appeared, and for weeks the town lived so vividly for me in Agnon's evocation of its physical and spiritual existence that I despaired of ever regaining the capacity to see it in any other terms than his. This cagily difficult parable, at once so arcane and so faithful to the immediacies of the here and now, seemed to arise from the deepest erotic and imaginative life of Jerusalem. Gemulah, especially, seemed a terrifying clue to the

neurasthenic pallor and resentful hysteria one sensed to be
endemic in the Orthodox women of the town, yet with all
this, the story managed also to enunciate a vision of universal malaise.

And there was something more in the tale. Though it
stood by itself as a literary work, it had behind it the
massed force of Agnon's preoccupations with a set of issues
and feelings central to his culture. Knowing Agnon's work,
one perceived in "Ido and Enam" the distillation of lifelong
attitudes and tensions. The anonymous narrator, as well as
Gamzu and Ginat, all seemed projections of various aspects
of Agnon himself. For Agnon's own quest, as a man and as
a writer, has involved a pursuit of the wholeness of past experience and a definition of a viable attitude to the quest
like those which engage his narrator. With both novellas in
mind, one is tempted to say that Agnon, like Rechnitz, has
been subject to the tidal pull of the submerged past, personal and historical; like Ginat, he has sought to detach
himself from the past in order to record it; like Gamzu, he
has at times sought to domesticate it; like the narrator, he
has struggled with his experience, an experience which reflects and clarifies the experience of his times. The specific
gravity of the tales can only be weighed against the background of his life and his times.

Those were times in which Agnon's compeers were striving to create a new world on the ruins of the old, in which
a past that was rapidly slipping into oblivion refused to sur-
render its hold over the spirit. The religious culture of the
East European *shtetl* (village), with its age-old sanctions,
was being superseded by the random secularism of the nineteenth century. And the social structure of the Jewish com-

munity was buckling under the pressure of economic change and political persecution. Zionism, with its dream of a Jewish state in Palestine, was meant to solve both difficulties. It would permit the renewal of Jewish culture on non-transcendental grounds, and it would avert political oppression by letting the Jews rule themselves.

Those who looked toward the future were hopeful; those who yearned for the past teetered on the brink of despair. Agnon is one of those who went through the motions of struggling toward the future, but it is clear that the past spoke more eloquently to him. His work records a sense of impotence in the face of time and change; it involves an effort to conjure necromantically, the realities of the obsolescent world toward which he yearns and to record the dilemmas that arise from such yearning. Finally, in parables like "Ido and Enam" and in a still later story, "Forevermore," he attempts to formulate an attitude toward the entire experience. The final perspective is neither so clear nor so definitive as Agnon's best work promises it could or would be. But it is a wide perspective, and one that, like these parables themselves, includes the greatest dilemmas of modern Jews and, in some respects, of all modern men: dilemmas that Agnon formulates from contemplation of his own historic experience and of the role of his literary activity in defining it.

[3]

Agnon is of Ben Gurion's generation—that is, the first generation of effective activists in the Zionist world. He was born Shmuel Yosef Czaczkes in 1888, seven years after the first wave of Zionist settlement in Palestine had begun, five years before the publication of Bialik's nostalgic Zionist poem, "To a Bird," and less than a decade before the first Zionist Congress, which defined the political aims of the Zionist movement. Agnon's birthplace was Buczacz, a middle-sized provincial town in the eastern sector of Austrian Galicia, an essentially Slavic province that had changed hands in the various partitions of Poland in the eighteenth century, and one whose native culture was dominated by the conventions and prejudices of the feudal Polish gentry and its Ukrainian peasantry. This meant an agriculture-based economy, a Roman Catholic culture, and a large measure of anti-Semitism among the peasants. At the same time, by virtue of its place in the Austro-Hungarian Empire, Galicia enjoyed a considerable measure of official enlightenment and "emancipation." Its public culture was German and its people enjoyed, from the latter third of the nineteenth century onward, a limited franchise within the political structure that centered in Vienna. The Jews, for the most part, remained rooted in their ancestral traditions but participated more fully in the life of secular society than did their brethren in Poland and Russia. Many of them attended secular schools, spoke German as well as Yiddish, and played some part in the political life of the community at large.

Agnon was born into a prosperous merchant family. It was deeply rooted in the religious tradition, but his mother was literate in German as well as in Yiddish, and Agnon himself was tutored in both German and Hebrew, though he studied the traditional religious texts as well. Altogether, the world of Agnon's youth seems nearly idyllic—compared, at least, with that of his East European contemporaries. His was, essentially, the "secure" world of Franz Josef's empire. Indeed, his background, for all its Hebraic, Orthodox, and incipient Zionist bias, seems to have been permeated by that diffuse sense of longing which characterized life in the Central European middle classes at the turn of the century—that hysteria of yearning which we know from Freud's case histories, as well as from the Schnitzleresque, Molnaresque literature that shades off within less than a generation into the anxious nightmares of Kafka and Musil.[7]

From his earliest days, Agnon wrote, producing prose and verse in Yiddish and Hebrew, and publishing works in both languages from the age of thirteen onward. The work that has been identified as his is full of *Schwärmerei* and romantic yearning; it is, as one of Agnon's critics has pointed out, rather characteristically neoromantic stuff, such as anyone in his circumstances might have written. Virtually nothing in the quality of that work—except possibly for his sense of the nuances of the Hebrew language—looks forward to the quality of his later work, though many of his later themes are clearly foreshadowed.

Quite early, too, Agnon made a Zionist commitment, presumably on sentimental rather than radical political grounds. Both Zionism and Hebraism were the prevailing modes of Jewish self-affirmation for the middle classes of the time. Such an affirmation was partly a response to the violent anti-Semitic outbursts in Russia and to the milder manifestation of anti-Semitism in Galicia. But it seems also to have served as a cultural substitute for the more religious modes that were rapidly being eroded by economic and social changes. Agnon would later—chiefly in "Young and

Old Together" and *A Simple Story*—excoriate the smugness and complacencies of such a Zionist identification. But in his youth he seems to have been mildly active in Zionism and to have accepted the spiritual sustenance it offered.

During the Second Aliyah—the wave of immigration to Palestine that came, chiefly from Russia, in the wake of the 1905 revolution—he made his way to Palestine. His immediate motives for doing so have never been explored. Some people have held that he was moved by the results of an election for the Austrian parliament, in which Jewish hopes had been dashed by fraudulent electoral practices and clear evidence of anti-Semitism. His most scathingly satiric novella "Young and Old Together" centers on that election and its spiritual atmosphere, so it may be presumed to have strongly affected him. For the most part, however, one has the impression—derived in part from his handling of characters in analogous circumstances—that he was carried along by a sentimental and nostalgic involvement with the Zionist idea. It is also likely that he was animated by the feeling that, if he was to be a Hebrew writer, he would have to root himself in the movement and the place where Hebrew would be revived.

Whatever his motives, this rather highly indulged, rather finicky Galician type found himself in Jaffa in 1907. According to all the evidence, he was an anomaly (yet not altogether an anomaly) among the brusque back-to-the-landers of the socialist camp and the fugitive householders of the burgher community. It was a time of ferment, seething with contradictions. Palestine was ruled by the Turks, who allowed Jews to settle, to acquire land, and to create their own institutions. But the Jewish Community was small, and it constituted only one of many small communities tolerated by the Turks and even granted extraterritorial privileges among them.

The Jews themselves were deeply split, moreover. There was an old, settled, Orthodox community, segments of which had lived in Palestine for centuries, and it opposed any effort to achieve political or economic autonomy or even to revive the Hebrew language, which was thought to be too sacred for mundane use. Pitted directly against the Orthodox, who adjured their coreligionists to await the coming of the Messiah, were the socialist activists: men who called for a transformation of the Jewish character and circumstances by the creation of a Jewish laboring community. Such men founded agricultural settlements, campaigned for the employment of Jewish labor in all branches of the economy, and appealed to their brethren abroad to join them in their endeavor. A third segment of the community was made up of householders, mainly petty-burgher types, who had either fled persecution abroad and merely wished to take up their lives as they had always lived them, or who had come as farmers but had regressed to the characteristic Jewish "livings": small shopkeeping, crafts, and the like.

It was a mixed scene, in language as well as ideology, in ethnic as well as political and religious terms. Individuals and groups came and went, and ideologies waxed and waned, as did political and literary "movements." Agnon was odd, but so were many others. In any case, he quickly found his place. He became the secretary for the journal published by the labor group in which Ben Gurion and the other fathers of the labor movement were active, and his literary ambitions were fostered by Berl Katznelson, one of the saints of the movement. He also had, from the earliest days, ties among the Orthodox and Hasidic groups: ties that were to deepen over the years, as he reverted more and more to the modes of the old Orthodoxy—an Orthodoxy which, we must always recall, he never completely abandoned in sentiment, if not in ritual practice.

As a writer, however, he stood very much alone. While his peers were busy excoriating the lassitude and corruption they saw in East European Jewry, Agnon was busy evoking the felicities and bereavements of the "community of the faithful," wherever it might be. Whereas Y. H. Brenner, the most distinguished of his peers, indulged in Dostoievskian orgies of self-laceration, harping on the social, moral, and metaphysical frailties of the Jews, Agnon sought to render the "whole loaf" of the aspiring soul's experience, creating delicate tales of love and fate within the framework of the traditional pieties (as these pieties continued to live in the rosy light of his imagination), or to portray his purely subjective experience on the margin of life in Tel Aviv–Jaffa. Unlike Brenner, who purged every shred of lyric loveliness from his prose, Agnon indulged himself in luxurious orchestrations of language and image, mating richly associative material from traditional sources with highly personal lyric themes. His theme was *aginut*, or bereavement—the word from which the title of his first major story, "Agunot" (1908), was derived and from which he took the pseudonym he has been known by ever since.[8] His characters tended to be innocents of one sort or another, full of mute yearning and subject to the vicissitudes of a fate that stemmed from internal weakness or external accident; the pathos of his tales arose from the characters' will-less submission to failure and frustration.

But Agnon was not long for this mode. By the time of World War I, the tenuous, exquisite tales were giving way to firmer, more objective work. In 1913, Agnon went to Germany, where he lived for more than a decade. There he became involved in the effort to transcribe the doomed traditions of Hasidism before they passed altogether out of existence. In the course of this effort, he developed a new sense of intellectual and spiritual fellowship—and, one infers, a sense of community such as he had never felt before. He formed ties with men like Martin Buber, the theologian and scholar; Gershom Scholem, a committed Zionist and a man destined to become the world's leading student of Jewish mysticism; and Salman Schocken, a businessman and publisher. Schocken became Agnon's patron and publisher, allowing him a regular stipend and bringing out all his works, beginning with a four-volume edition inaugurated in 1931.

His German years were very productive for Agnon. He was exposed to a new, exciting milieu and confirmed in his literary interests. While in Germany, Agnon married the daughter of a distinguished Königsberg family; together, the Agnons became part of a fairly large community of Hebrew writers and scholars congregated in Germany after the war.

Agnon, his wife, and their two children returned to Palestine in 1924 and settled in a suburb of Jerusalem, where they have lived, with short intermissions, ever since. Secure in reputation and more or less sustained by his publisher's allowance, he has lived apart: always in touch with the academic and literary communities, in which his German-Jewish friends have played a vital part, but largely withdrawn into steady contemplation and expression of the kinds of experience that are closest to his heart. He obviously follows events in his country with interest, and he has from time to time taken strong, fairly nationalistic stands on current issues. But for the most part he has remained aloof from public life, adopting a firmly ironic attitude toward politics, which he treats as part of the gray round of meaningless movement that for him is the modern world. Indeed, his sense of the essential absurdity of politics is expressed in a series of mordantly satiric stories entitled "The Book of the State."

[4]

If Agnon has withdrawn from the world of action, he has not withdrawn from the world of fact. Already, in his Berlin period, he had produced a series of tales rooted in the actuality of the waning East European *shtetl*. That sequence of stories, fables, and novellas is remarkable for its vivid evocation of the past and for its immediate empathy with its people and their modes of being within it. These stories culminated, in 1931, in a long piece of prose fiction —*The Bridal Canopy*—which was immediately hailed as *the* epic representation of Jewish life in Eastern Europe in the premodern period.[9] *The Bridal Canopy* is an elaborate frame story, on the model of *Don Quixote,* with strong affinities to Mendele's *Benjamin the Third* and Sholem Aleichem's *Tevye the Dairyman*. A folk tale organized around the travels of its hero, Reb Yudel, *The Bridal Canopy* projects the spirit—but also the historical actuality—of a period in which even miracles still remained conceivable. Yet it cannot be said to be a mere exercise in nostalgia; conjuring a lost world, it never allows us to lose sight of the necessary and inevitable decline of that world.

The Bridal Canopy represents Agnon's emergence from the twilight of the early tales. I find it at times tedious, labored, and too sustainedly coy. It displays his remarkable architectonic gifts, however, and it seems to have confronted him with the crucial problem of history, of the relation between the past and the present, which forms the central concern of the late parables and of his major fiction. Even as he was summoning up a vision of the old world of the "fathers," he seems to have begun to come to grips with his own problematical relation to it. Agnon's later novels deal with the impact of that world's decline upon people like himself who must bear the body of its death. His own historical situation becomes the focus of his work—a situation in which the individual remains sentimentally bound to a decaying social and cultural order which magnetizes his sensibility and prevents him from shaping a satisfactory life in a changing universe. As Susan is to Rechnitz, and Gemulah to Gamzu, so the *shtetl* and the entire tribal past are to the Agnon hero, who is caught between two worlds and belongs to neither. Though he has left Reb Yudel behind, the ancestral past continues to serve Agnon as the foundation of his consciousness and even of his judgment, as a source of stability and the basis of his alienation from modernity. His *judgment* of that foundation remains achingly obscure, but his novelistic manipulation of it is almost uniformly impressive.

In orienting his fiction as he does, Agnon began to crystallize a set of issues that had been implicit in Zionism from the outset. The history of Zionism is marked by a deep ambivalence toward the centers of Jewish life in the Diaspora and toward the concept of the Diaspora itself. On the one hand the Diaspora represented a negative condition: exile, persecution, backwardness. Zionism, in this perspective, figured as the resurrection of a lost but desiderated reality. Thus, the Diaspora, the Diaspora Jew, and the Diasporic way of life became hateful. Yet for the individual, the Diaspora was home; his primal sympathies were invested there. "Man," the poet Saul Tchernichowsky was to write, "is no more than the soil of a little land." If, for the individual Zionist, the Diaspora was hateful because it afforded little contact with the soil, if it was thought to cut one off from nature, from life, and from normalcy itself, one's human nature and experience were richly implicated in it.

Modern Hebrew literature, bound up with the Zionist cause, has been wracked by this ambivalence. The very language of the new literature implies a negation of the mother tongue; to cultivate Hebrew meant, on the whole, to reject Yiddish, to forge a new instrument designed to create a new set of responses, a new frame for the brave old-new world in Zion. The very language, as a literary instrument, implied a struggle to overthrow the old, "black Orthodox," reactionary order of *shtetl* life. Even when—at the time of the "Hebrew Renaissance" in the last third of the nineteenth century—the espousal of the language came to symbolize an identification with the ongoing life of the folk and an effort to preserve such elements of the old communality as could be saved, the effort was in a sense contaminated by its origins. Historically, modern Hebrew literature stemmed from an attempt by members of the emergent Jewish middle class in Germany (and later in Austria and Galicia) to identify themselves with the forces of change—of "progress"—which threatened utterly to undermine the bases of the old order of life in the Jewish community. For the old order had been embedded in the quasifeudal structure of East European society; its religious and communal systems were rooted in that structure and were directly menaced by the modes of rationalist thought and action implicit in the social and economic changes that lay behind the European Enlightenment itself.

Agnon not only refused to join in the habitual denigration of the old order, but also came to perceive with growing clarity the conflict between the traditional modes of experience and the rationalist, progressivist attitudes that pervaded the Zionist ideology. He came, moreover, to have a sense of the irrationality at work in the heart of the progressive processes of modernism and tried to relate the larger patterns of that irrationality to the kind of irrationality he saw at work in the individual Jew. He perceived in the soul of the individual Jew, in his struggle to be free of the limitations of the past, a tropism toward the very past he was trying to escape—a tropism that doomed him to an inner fragmentation and outer alienation, and yet linked him to a transcendent realm that gave meaning to life and the world. The history of Agnon's own development is a history of increasing—yet often inadequate—self-consciousness with regard to the personal and historical conflicts that are implicit in the changing communal experience.

His novels, after *The Bridal Canopy*, reflect the growth

of this self-consciousness. *A Simple Story* (1935) deals with a passive young man born into a bourgeois family in Galicia at the turn of the century, and with the crisis he undergoes as he proves unable and unwilling to assume the roles forced upon him there.[10] As Rechnitz yearns for Susan, so Hershel of *A Simple Story* dreams of Blumah Nacht, his childhood sweetheart, but cannot assert himself and take her; he goes mad when his flighty country wife, foisted on him by his parents, bears him a son. For him the madhouse is a place of peace, a refuge from the nightmare reality of his life. The failure of Hershel's personal will is a perfect mirror of the failure of will in his entire environment. He feels that his father is "more" than he is, and is dimly aware that his father's fathers were more than his father; the entire community seems to have lost touch with the sources of its vitality, to have become a stagnant backwater of vanity, passivity, evasion, and greed.

The next novel directly confronts the final deterioration of that milieu. *A Guest for the Night* (1939)—written in a narrative mode somewhat reminiscent of the expressionist fiction of the twenties—is about a man who has settled in Palestine and returns full of nostalgia some time after World War I to his home town in Galicia, only to find it in a state of utter decay.[11] In *Yesteryear* (1945), the third novel after *The Bridal Canopy*, Agnon travels backward in time, exploring the inner dislocation of an individual who seeks to solve the problem of exile by emigrating to Palestine during the Second Aliyah and tries to recreate a tradition of heroism by joining in the effort to resuscitate the folk in its own land.[12] Yitzhak Kummer (who is the great-grandson of Reb Yudel of *The Bridal Canopy*) takes the Zionist dream seriously; he imbibes the ideals of the Zionist pamphlets which he reads in his father's store and rebels against the stagnation and corruption that surround him —the same stagnation that had engulfed Hershel, the hero of *A Simple Story*, before him. By emigrating to Palestine, Kummer believes that he will be able to rehabilitate himself, but it turns out that, for all his apparent activity— "movement" is a better word—Yitzhak is as passive as Hershel and just as subject to regressive longings.

There is one important difference, however. The failure of Yitzhak's will is accompanied by a corrosive awareness of his ancestry, and specifically of Reb Yudel, the Hasid who had emigrated to Palestine under very different circumstances, in a very different frame of mind. Reb Yudel had "gone up" to the Holy Land after the good Lord had, by a miracle, provided his daughters with a dowry and absolved him from the struggle for survival in an utterly resistant environment. Yitzhak thinks of himself as walking in his grandfather's footsteps, but is haunted by the sense that Providence no longer watches over him, that his life can no longer be what Reb Yudel's was. In this frame of mind, he lives out his gruesome fate, slowly, almost without conflict, reverting to the occupations, the habits, and, the rituals of his forefathers. Having come to Palestine to be a pioneer among pioneers, he ends up a member of the parasitic, old-guard community of Meah Shearim in Jerusalem, betrothed to the daughter of a Hungarian religious fanatic. He dies of the rabies communicated to him one sweltering afternoon by a dog that lurches at him from under the gabardine of a ranting preacher with whom his father-in-law is imaginatively linked.

Yitzhak is an Isaac meaninglessly sacrificed to ancestral passions. He has been conditioned to act according to a set of roles and patterns that are passing out of existence, and so, like most of Agnon's heroes, he finds himself filled with chaotic longings for objects concealed from his waking consciousness. Like Shifra, his bride, and his mother before her, these objects ultimately point beyond this world. But they are mediated through a firm sociological pattern in which he no longer can find a place. His destiny, much like those of Rechnitz, Gamzu, and Hershel, works itself out in terms of an erotic compulsion.

Yitzhak is himself responsible for the madness of the mad dog that destroys him. It is he who had inadvertently dribbled the words "mad dog" in paint on the dog's back, and it is this label that leads people to hound and harass the poor beast until it does go mad, in fact as well as in fancy. The long mad-dog episode is an allegory on allegories and on pariahdom itself. But Balak, the mad dog, is a symbol of Yitzhak's sexuality and the sexual implications of his relation to his forebears.

In *Yesteryear*, Agnon clinched his formulation of the central dilemma of his world. *A Guest for the Night*, anticipating the Holocaust, had confronted with finality the shattering of the old frame of reference. One cannot go home again, because the old society no longer exists; all that remains to the narrator of the novel, as to the narrator of "Ido and Enam," is the key to a ruined sanctuary and the possibility of vivifying the past in the creative imagination.

The present, then, is unbearable, and the past will not die: this is the dilemma in which the typical Agnon hero is caught. He tends to be disoriented, hanging between the madness and meaninglessness of the world as it is and his deep bondage to a past which neutralizes the present even as it alienates him from it.

[5]

Much of Agnon's short fiction since the early 1930's has been concerned with representing either the radically equivocal states of being that arise when one is unwillingly possessed by the past or when one willfully tries to recapture it. These stories fall roughly into three groups. There is the usually brief nightmarish tale, rather Kafkaesque in technique, that renders the experience of an individual whose life is disrupted by an onrush of incomprehensible events obscurely related to his wishes and fears. Then there is the expressionist tale, directly related to the last volume of Hermann Broch's novel *The Sleepwalkers*, but with affinities to the art of Frank Wedekind, Robert Musil, and even the early Bertold Brecht. These present an utterly fragmented and demented outer world which often reflects a disrupted inner world but which has independent validity as an image of chaos and upheaval. And finally there is the self-conscious parable of a quest, like "Ido and Enam," in which characters consciously and unconsciously seek out ways of resuscitating the old, sanctified modes of existence, trying to order their experience and find goodness, beauty, and truth in a wayward, desperate present.

One notes the persistence, in all three types of story, of certain motifs, involving what we might call an Agnon figure—that is, involving a writer or scholar (like Ginat, Gamzu, and Rechnitz) who deliberately tries to contact, record, or preserve a lost or elusive reality. All these characters share an alienation from ordinary experience; all of them pursue their interest in relative or complete isolation, often with a Magian intensity. Some, like Rechnitz, are driven by obscure cravings which stem from an aberrant or displaced sexuality and which make them simultaneously demonic in their work and passive in the circumstances of everyday life. Curiously, however, these special characters are not essentially different from the more commonplace figures who move through Agnon's work. Agnon's ordinary protagonist is a little man who tends toward a bewildered incomprehension of the things that happen to him. He is—one might say—an archetype of bewilderment.

This figure represents the peculiar strength as well as the peculiar limitation of Agnon's achievement. He has been compared to Kafka's heroes, just as the modernist tales about him have been compared in style and form to Kafka's work. If one seeks analogies in modern literature, however, one would do better to look to Faulkner, whose characters remain caught up in the traditions of the old South and continue to live within its mythos without being able to evolve viable relationships in the world which has supplanted it. The difference is that Faulkner's people respond to this situation with glorified self-dramatization in postures of defeat, while Agnon's people respond to their circumstances with Chaplinesque incomprehension and a reflexive shrug of the shoulders, in which wit and imbecility coincide.[13]

Indeed, as Agnon moves further and further away from the dead *shtetl* culture, as he contemplates the failure of the Zionist effort either to reincarnate the *shtetl* or to resurrect

the religious commonwealth of ancient Israel, as he crystal-
lizes a sense of the ugliness, the fragmentation, and the sys-
tematic irrelevance to human desire of the modern world,
his protagonists slouch ever more deeply, groan ever more
pathetically, fall ever more habitually into the clichés of
self-denigration. The voice in which he speaks is the voice
of the *shlemiehl;* the crinkle of self-pity and the quaver of
self-doubt define its range.

There are anomalies here. The idiom of Agnon's novels
is pietistic, the logic seems rigorous, and the erudition—rabbinic—is vast; yet, in fact, the logic is shuffle-gaited, and
the erudition is irrelevant to the ongoing concerns of life.
Agnon tries desperately to think things out, but his very
idiom exposes a failure of thought. The marvelously nu-
anced prose, if its rhetoric and syntax are examined closely,
reflects a dramatic inability to define causes or to measure
time and space significantly. Its very flow and cadence take
on the quality of a universal *krechtz,* or groan. In view of
Agnon's own "Zionist" choice to write in Hebrew, and in
view of his massive contribution to the development of
modern Hebrew as a literary medium, it is supremely
ironic that his language should often seem a transmogrified,
quintessential rendering in Hebrew of something native to
Yiddish at its most reflexive. His prose is a language never
heard on land or sea, impeccably Hebraic and yet molded
in the cadence of another mode—a Yiddish one—another
language, another form of consciousness.[14] Indeed, the
pleasures which Agnon's prose style affords are themselves
a symptom of the underlying difficulty. So much is invested by Agnon in the language that, instead of serving as
a pane of clear glass through which we might envision a

world, it often seems one of those finely wrought products of vitreous art in which figures are etched into the glass itself. His language ultimately points back to itself, rather than outward into an objectified fictional universe. There is an objective attunement to the outer world and its problems. But there is also always the self-regarding, aestheticizing intrusion of Agnon's sensibility. I insist, in contrast to some of Agnon's more sensitive readers, that he is not a mere aesthete; his work is too rich and too deeply engaged with some aspects of reality for him to be seen as one. But I hold that he does not achieve a vigorous substantive engagement with the ultimate implications of his experience.

In a sense, his range is too narrow, and the historical scope of his fiction fails to make up for the limited span of experience it encompasses. Agnon lacks gusto, and so do his characters. Their inherent passivity—their incapacity to engage in passionate struggle—oppresses the reader and, in the end, makes for a lack of conviction as to the integrity of the total vision. One always feels that something is left out—that some range of energies and impulses remains unconfronted.

The common comparison to Kafka suggests one source of the weakness. Within the psychic smog of Kafka's world there is a tensed, even compulsive will to be, to achieve, to escape. Kafka's obsession with his father, with authority in general, is unpleasant in its clinical baldness, but out of it there seems to grow a tenacity of will and a countering fixity of guilt. Such tension is largely absent in Agnon. In psychological terms, his characters are obsessed not with the father, but with the mother, and the result is a propensity to undergo life in a labile, feminine mode. Aggression is deeply suppressed, and the scope of erotic imagination is limited. These things are probably in part a function of the cultural presuppositions of Agnon's imaginative world. But they are in part a function of his failure energetically to probe the psychological underpinnings of his characters—or, finally, his own.

More damaging, ultimately, is the underlying irresolution in Agnon's attitude toward his material. The late parables bespeak the hopelessness of attempting to embody the high aims and ravening dreams of the Rechnitzes, Ginats, and Gamzus. Yet they may also be said to constitute a kind of elegiac celebration of that fond, foolish effort—the only effort worth making in this shattered world. It is surely no accident that Agnon's first novel had *Don Quixote* in its background; *The Bridal Canopy* and all the work that follows are riddled with a Cervantesque ambivalence toward the figure of the hero—treating him as saint and fool, martyr and "fall guy," be he Reb Yudel or Ginat-Gamzu-Agnon. It is the sort of ambivalence that mocks the objects of its heroes' desire, and it accounts in part for the quality of unpleasantness in Agnon's work. The price of the remarkable lyricism of the pathetic comedy of his own and his people's journey through the anterooms of modernity into the center of its hell is a faint nastiness, an uneasy afterstench of self-indulgence which precludes wisdom, passion, and even the larger energy of a truly hellish ordeal.

Yet one is drawn to Agnon's vision and to the intricacies and bafflements which his own irresolution begets. For it is out of the effort to reconcile his conflicting attitudes of irony and celebration that the rich fabric of his work is woven—work, finally, which seeks to embody in itself the elusive wholeness that is the object of man's desire. That wholeness may in fact be unattainable, but from Agnon's work—as from Ginat's published Enamite hymns—there shines, for those who can glimpse it, the light of the higher yearning. Each of his readers must decide whether this light can suffice.[15]

[2]
The Whole Loaf: Agnon's Tales
of the Ancestral World

About a third of Agnon's work directly reflects the culture of the *shtetl* before its final decline.[1] Entirely devoted to a limited range of experience in the century preceding Agnon's birth, such work takes the form of folk tales in the idiom of the faithful who enjoyed the "whole loaf" of experience within the ancestral tradition. The civilization of the *shtetl* had defined itself for centuries almost entirely in terms of that tradition. Agnon attempts to render the quality of experience within it.

[1]

If one seeks a spiritual center of gravity within the Agnonic *shtetl*, one finds it in the pervasive feeling that, ultimately, mortality holds no terrors for its folk. The denizens of Agnon's traditionalistic tales live in a world where pain and loss are pervasive. There are pogroms and persecutions; there is poverty; there is the final fact of death. But pain and loss can be placed in a larger conception of moral order in the cosmos, of an implicit logic in events. One craves the good things of the life of this world, but one is perpetually aware of their transience. The real life—the true, the intelligible world—is elsewhere. Though one does not negate the immediate conditions of one's existence—the tradition, after all, is essentially not otherworldly—one knows its limits and strives within the established order of faith to transcend it.

The culture of the *shtetl* had its upheavals. The life of East European Jewry between 1770 and 1880 was stormy, even in relatively peaceful Galicia. But Agnon is not occupied with its upheavals. His tales of the ancestral world are meticulous in historical detail, touching again and again upon the tensions and disruptions of the times. The emphasis, however, is not on the conflict in and for itself, but on its effect on the individual caught up in it. What really interests Agnon is the way individuals accommodate themselves to the stresses of life within village culture.[2]

Those who celebrate Agnon as an epic writer do so because of the lucidity with which he conjures the actualities of the lost village past. And, indeed, his technique is highly objective. He writes folk tales full of people, things, events, evoking a world where the daily round of actions and responses unfolds at a leisurely pace. The emphasis, however, is not on the objective order, but rather on the strain of feeling that informs the lives of its people. The prevailing tone of the tales—even the broadly comic ones—is lyric in the extreme. Agnon tunes in on a delicate, tremulous strain of feeling that, he implies, suffused the culture at large and came to fruition in individuals. And the consciousness of these individuals is ordered by the governing patterns of consciousness in their civilization.

What characterizes the denizens of Agnon's *shtetl* is a radical limitation of individual consciousness and a peculiar passivity in confronting the conditions of their lives. There is conflict, but it is always defined in conventional terms.

There is struggle, but the struggle is rarely ultimate. Agnon's village folk never strike out boldly against the things that undo them, and they rarely reflect on themselves or the immediate causes of their anguish. When they do reflect on their circumstances, everything is referred back to the governing order of things—to God, to galut (exile, Diaspora), to schemes of sin and punishment that imply divine governance. The world is seen wholly in terms of the system of ideas and images that order their lives. Both nature and history are grasped in such terms.

The effect, aesthetically, is that of certain folk drawings, where stars modulate into Sabbath candles, and the world of nature arranges itself around a *sukkah* (tabernacle) or the Ark of the Covenant. The inner life is treated in a similar fashion. The life of the feelings is mediated through sets of prototypical patterns and analogues. To long for one's lost love is to be an *agunah*, that is, a grass widow, who is bereaved in this life; to sit among the ruins of one's shop is to be like the city that sat desolate.

The people of Agnon's tales of *shtetl* life have little individuality in our sense of the word. They are discrete beings, possessed of particular qualities and sharply distinguished from each other. They lack self-consciousness, however, and rarely turn in upon themselves. They never hurl themselves against the existing order of things, and they therefore have little inwardness in the way people in modern fiction ordinarily do. What they do have is an intensified experience of a clearly delimited range of feeling, which Agnon echoes and amplifies to the fullest. They are given to a deeply felt sense of ineffable longing, ineffable loss, ineffable pleasure in longing and loss—which Agnon devotes his formidable gifts to evoking. The most striking thing about his shorter tales is the lapidary elegance with which they dramatize the experience of relatively passive individuals, reaching beyond the flesh and the world. Even the comic tales, with their emphasis on incongruity and happy endings, are infused with a muted melancholy quaver and a constant sense of the something beyond.

Agnon's early tales are remarkably consistent in their evocation of these qualities. Though they vary in theme, in nuance of background, and—subtly—in technique, they share the peculiar beauty and harmony he casts on *shtetl* types in describing their response to the pain of existence. The tales this chapter discusses represent, in a way, variations on a unifying theme: the theme of loss, in a field of experience where loss can be undergone in a larger context, where harmonization of discord is possible, as well as an extraordinary aesthetization of pain. Such aesthetization of experience, but also of the spirit of the *shtetl* as Agnon sees it, is perhaps the most striking quality of these tales. It is also their most drastic limit.

[2]

"Agunot" (1908), Agnon's first major tale, sets the tone for the later tales; it is a kind of prelude to his life's work. Attuned to the moods of the *shtetl* as he apprehended them, though not specifically concerned with its milieu, it established the thematic and sentimental patterns that have dominated his work.

"Agunot" is a tale of thwarted love. Its heroine, Dinah, is a girl of fairy-tale loveliness, reared tenderly by a father who wishes to marry her to a renowned scholar. She falls in love, however, with an artist who has been commissioned to build an ark for the Torah scrolls in the house of study over which her husband is to preside. Ben Uri, the artist, is too deeply absorbed in his task to take notice of her, and she marries Ezekiel, a prodigious scholar her father has imported for her from abroad. Ezekiel in turn loves Freidele, a simple *shtetl* girl, the daughter of his father's housekeeper, who returns his love. After the marriage, Dinah dreams of Ben Uri, Ezekiel of Freidele.

The marriage does not work. Ahiezer, Dinah's father, who had gone to Jerusalem "to rebuild and refound her, from her ruins," acknowledges that his intentions have not prospered. He takes Dinah to the Rabbi, who had known of Dinah's predilections, and the Rabbi undoes the marriage knot. Ahiezer leaves Jerusalem, and Dinah goes with him. One night, the Rabbi dreams a disquieting dream, and after dreaming it once again, takes up a pilgrim's staff and wallet and goes out into exile with a view to "repairing" the bereaved souls, like Ben Uri's and Dinah's, that wander in droves through limbo.

The tale is suffused with thwarted yearning. Its basic motifs are sounded at the very outset:

It is said: A thread of grace is spun and drawn from the deeds of Israel, and the Holy One, blessed be He, Himself, in His glory, sits and weaves a prayer shawl all grace and all mercy for the Congregation of Israel to enfold herself in. Radiant in the light of her beauty she glows, even in these the lands of her exile, as she did in her youth, in her Father's house, in the temple of her Sovereign and the city of sovereignty, Jerusalem. When He, of Ineffable Name, sees her, that she has been neither sullied nor stained even here, in the lands of her oppressors, He—as it were—leans toward her and says, "Behold, thou art fair, my love, behold thou art fair." And this is the secret of the power and the glory and the exaltation and the tenderness in love which fill the heart of every man in Israel.

But there are times—alas!—when some temptation creeps up and snaps a thread in the loom. Then the prayer shawl is damaged. Evil spirits hover about it, . . . and tear it to shreds. At once a sense of shame assails all Israel, and they know they are naked. Their days of rest are wrested from them, their feasts are fasts, and their lot is dust instead of luster. At that hour the Congregation of Israel strays abroad in her anguish, crying, "Strike me, scourge me, strip away my veils from me!" Her beloved has slipped away, and she, seeking Him, cries, "If ye find my beloved, what shall ye say unto Him? That I am afflicted with love." And this affliction leads to direst melancholy which persists—Mercy shield us!—until from the heavens above He breathes down upon us strength of spirit to repent, and to muster deeds that are a pride to their doer, and again to draw forth the thread of grace before the Lord.[3]

By setting the star-crossed lovers in a field of rich traditional associations, Agnon achieves a fine lyric resonance. It is no mere accident that sends bereaved souls into the world seeking their mates, but rather a near-cosmic fatality. Ben Uri and Dinah, Ezekiel and Freidele, and also Ahiezer and Jerusalem itself, figure within a prototypical pattern of loss, associated as they are with both the Shulamite of the Song of Songs and the Congregation of Israel in its distress. The Rabbi who takes up his pilgrim's staff to wander in the world is the prototype of the saint who wanders in the darkness of life, seeking to right its incomprehensible wrongs. Jerusalem is not merely a city, but *the* city, land of the pious heart's desire, whence men wander in gloom,

coerced by the mysterious workings of chance or of fate—
of the sin that, in the formulation of the tale's opening,
"catches a thread in the loom." The rest of the world is
outer darkness, Diaspora, exile—banishment, ultimately,
from both terrestrial delight and the joy of existence in the
light of the divine presence.[4]

The title of the tale clinches the sense of universal bereavement. The *agunah* was the grass widow of the Jewish
Law, which had no statute of limitations in family matters,
so that a woman whose husband had disappeared could not
remarry till he had been proved dead—or sent her a di-
vorce. As it happens, every soul in this tale is in a state of
aginut—including the mourning figure of the Holy Spirit
(*shekhinah*) who appears to the old Rabbi in his dream,
cooing mournfully like a dove. Everyone in the tale is an
agunah, fatally bound to an inaccessible love object and unable to break out of the "web." And though there clearly is
a cause, no one need struggle to know it. Whether the
cause is an accident of human history or of an inevitability
of the transcendent Law does not matter. It merely is. And
the sadness of it is unspeakably lovely, its loveliness unspeakably sad.

[3]

"The Crooked Made Straight" (1912), Agnon's next
major tale, is less penumbral than "Agunot."[5] Its action is
more directly recounted; its characters are sharper and
more vivid. It is a moral tale that projects an analogous
mood far more obliquely. Its moral is stated at the outset:
"The sage hath said, 'Wealth is less substantial than vanity,' . . . to make it known how frail and insubstantial

money is, since it has no intrinsic value. . . . By its very nature . . . [it] evanesces . . . [and] for the least of reasons
. . . it is lost." [6] The story itself recounts

a series of events involving a certain man, Menashe Haim by
name, . . . who fell from prosperity . . . and was driven . . .
into transgression. How he was oppressed . . . but did not op-
press others, and [therefore] came into his own in his death
and enjoyed a name and a memorial among the living, as is set
forth at length . . . within the tale. It is of him and the likes of
him that it is written, "And then they shall atone for their
sins"; to which our rabbis added . . . , "They shall atone for
their sins through suffering." [7]

The tale tells of the progressive impoverishment of a decent but childless shopkeeping couple to the point where
the husband must take to the road as a certified beggar. We
watch the husband's deterioration from a householder's dignity to rank mendicancy. Menashe Haim sinks so low that,
at the very moment he has enough alms in hand to justify
his heading homeward, he sells his credentials to a profes-
sional beggar and then eats and drinks himself insensate.
When he awakes, he finds that all his money has been sto-
len and takes to the road again, now as a common pariah.

Time passes. Finally, the other beggar drinks himself to
death, and Menashe Haim, whose documents he carries,
comes to be thought of as dead. By the time Menashe Haim
has worked his way home again, Kraindel Charney, his
long-suffering wife—who has languished patiently, first as
an *agunah* and then as a widow—has finally remarried and
is celebrating the birth of a son. Stunned, Menashe Haim
takes to the road again. Finally, after much wandering, he
stumbles into the cemetery where his wife has erected a

monument to "him"—that is, to the beggar who has been mistaken for him. Menashe Haim, exhausted, dies there, and is buried by a kindly gravedigger alongside the monument that bears his name. In the end, he benefits from the prayers and offerings his still loving wife tenders in his name.

The imaginative emphasis of the tale is on the grotesquerie of Menashe Haim's life and death and the final, graveyard peace he achieves. At the center of the story is the selling of the begging certificate at a nightmarish fair, with its monstrous distractions and its deafening din. A beggar in shrouds sings mournfully of how he returned from the other world to find his door shut against him. A woman sitting on a pile of rags keens her misery as an *agunah*.

The fair seems to externalize something in Menashe Haim himself. What Menashe Haim sees at the fair anticipates what will happen to him in life. It suggests, moreover, that the "real" world is a nightmare of vanity, mortality, disincarnation. When Menashe Haim gorges and gluttonizes at the inn, we recoil from the sour taste in his mouth and his sodden flesh. The death of Menashe Haim's double is still more revolting.

Altogether, there is a sense of the hideousness of the flesh —and of its deathliness. The flesh is equated with selfhood, with a kind of death of the spirit. At the end, Menashe Haim is in a sense reborn in the spirit, having purged himself through suffering and remorse. Thus, the tale bears out its "argument." We perceive the mutability of a happiness rooted in the world and the flesh. Menashe Haim is happy only when, insensate with suffering, he finds repose among the tombstones and comes to rest underground. Like "Agunot," "The Crooked Made Straight" suggests that the common condition of mankind is indeed a condition of disenfleshment without disenchantment, of pariahdom without final degradation, of *aginut* without desperation—only of incessant, muted desire.

Nor is the disenfleshment unpleasant. Menashe Haim, all passion spent, seems happier underground than anywhere else. But even underground and passionless, he has not stopped yearning. He still wants the tenderness of Kraindel Charney's love. From our point of view as readers of the tale, he gets them. Kraindel Charney lays offerings on his grave.

[4]

"The Legend of the Scribe" (1919), has a more positive emphasis, though it too moves toward dissolution and death.[8] "The Crooked Made Straight" is a moral fable with Gothic touches, "The Legend of the Scribe" an idyl of love within the Law, with a moment of hallucination at the end. It suggests how fantasy and feeling can indeed be embodied in a marriage of tender beauty and essential innocence, even as they can be released in a moment of peculiar delight that neutralizes the horror of death. The opening sets the tone for what follows:

These are the events of Raphael the scribe. Raphael the scribe was a wholly pious man, who used to prepare Torah scrolls and phylacteries and *mezuzot* in perfect sanctity. It was the way of householders who were afflicted with childlessness, God help us, and whose wives had been taken from them, to come to Raphael and say to him, "You know, good Raphael,

what we are and what we will be. I had hoped to see my sons
and the sons of my sons come to you and ask you to indite for
them their phylacteries in their time. But now, alas, I am desolate and forlorn. My wife, whom I had hoped to await
through the days and the years in the heavens above—my wife
has suddenly passed on before me, and left me to nothing but
tears. Perhaps you could bring yourself, good Raphael, to prepare a Torah scroll for me, in accordance, with my means,
such as they are, as the hand of the Lord is kindly upon you.
. . ." And Raphael the scribe would sit himself down and prepare him a scroll, that he might leave behind him some memory, some monument in Israel.[9]

The action of the tale is radically simple. We learn how
Raphael lived and worked, of the quality of his relationship
to his wife, of their childlessness, and of the irony of his
preparing Torah scrolls for the childless. And we learn of
Miriam's tender yearning, how she prayed that the Lord
might bless her womb, even as she tenderly ministered to
the children of others. Then we see how their life is disrupted by Miriam's sudden death and learn how Raphael
decides to prepare a Torah scroll in her memory. We
watch Raphael immerse himself in the ritual of scroll-writ-
ing. And we watch him, when he has completed his labor
of love, as he dances with the scroll, which he has decked
out in a cover made of Miriam's wedding dress, and is carried back to that Simhat Torah (Festival of Rejoicing in
the Law) long ago, when he was a boy and first joined the
men in the dance. He recalls how Miriam, hardly more
than a child, came to kiss his Torah scroll and, having
burned his jacket with her candle, was engaged to him. He
sings as he dances, singing the song and dancing the dance

he had danced then, confounding the now and the then in the song. Though Miriam is dead and her wedding dress adorns the Torah scroll he has written in memory of her, he reaches into the closet to find the dress. Having looked and having found only a bag of earth from the Holy Land —the very earth he had placed in Miriam's grave—he dies, and is found with the wedding dress over his face.

The tale is remarkable in its capturing of the tenderness that informs Raphael and Miriam's life together, and in its modulating into the quiet ecstasy of Raphael's final dance. We have the sense that for Raphael, within the containing forms of the tradition, the life of love and the life of the Law are continuous, not dichotomous; for once, Eros and civilization do not collide. The one feeds the other, and is fed by it. To be a scribe, monastically dedicated to the transcription of the Law, and to be a man and a husband are not disjunctive; the kissing, the touching, the singing, the dancing—and also the fasting, the praying, the self-containment—that signify one aspect of life inform the other as well. Agnon captures the process whereby such congruence is made possible in his account of the Sabbath encounter between man and wife.

While Miriam stands in the ritual bath, Raphael tarries in the house of prayer. When she comes home from the bath, she puts on garments as lovely as those of a bride on the day of her nuptials and stands in front of the mirror. At that moment it seems to her that the days of her girlhood have returned; she sees the inn that had stood at the crossroads, where lords and ladies used to come and cattle merchants used to lodge—where she had lived with her mother and her father and with Raphael, the lord of her youth, and she remembers for a moment the veil her mother had made for her marriage. For a moment, she thinks of adorning herself for her husband. But then she sees, glancing at her out of the mirror, the sampler she had made as a girl, which now hangs on the wall opposite—the pair of lions standing within it, their mouths open [to utter the glories of the Lord]. She recoils from her thought. "The earth is the Lord's and the fullness thereof!"

So that when Raphael returns from his devotions and beholds his wife in her loveliness, . . . he draws near to whisper endearments in her ear. But when he reaches her, he sees the Lord's name reflected in the glass . . . and reads with reverence, "I shall hold Him always before me." Then he shuts his eyes and turns from her, to honor the Lord in his holiness. They part in silence. He sits in one corner of the room, reading the Zohar and its commentaries, and she sits in another, saying her prayers, until sleep comes to dim their eyes. They rise and take the copper bucket with the copper fish engraved on its bottom, and they wash their hands for their evening prayers.[10]

There is nothing puritanical in Miriam's failure to adorn herself as a bride. She is intrinsically a bride. Consciousness of her place in God's world makes her one. Her memory of girlhood becomes part of her consciousness of a larger pattern to which she belongs. To see the sampler on the wall, with its evocation of the greater context of her existence, is to realize her essential form. Raphael and Miriam go to bed, like other couples. But their doing so seems an aspect of a larger reality of which they are a part.

What Agnon suggests is a kind of ladder of love, on which the movement from one plane of love to another is achieved without negation of the "lower" planes. It is this that makes possible the peculiar equanimity with which Raphael experiences the final hallucination, which is potentially so dissonant and yet so filled with a sense of the tenuousness of life.

In fact, the underlying life of the tale seems to stem from a paradox. What Raphael and Miriam are—and love—intimates a pattern of transcendence and is contained in a way of life that is the earthly vehicle for that pattern. But the delicate balance of feeling, its perfect poise, arises within life, and consists of the shifting, time-bound mortal realities: the human feelings which, however they are caught up in the governing pattern of transcendence, are subject to mortality and can themselves be disintegrated, under the pressure of experience, into the time-bound realities which have constituted them.

But even such disintegration need not finally disrupt. At the end of his life, Raphael is still dancing the dance of the Law with which his meaningful life as man and husband began. And, though *we* may perceive it differently, Raphael's experience remains integral. His dance of death is his dance of life. As he dances, his consciousness, which carries him back to the past, before the beginning of his love, is moving backward and forward at once, to what has become a timeless past and to what will be a timeless future, in death. But in both directions he moves toward the unifying goal of his life. And that goal is both in life and beyond life.

[5]

"The Outcast," published in the same year as "The Legend of the Scribe," renders a similar theme more elaborately.[11] It is concerned, not with the quiet felicity of a traditional marriage, but with the torment and upheaval in the life of a boy torn between two traditions. Set at the time of the first appearance of Hasidism in eastern Galicia, it is more concrete in social and historical detail than any of the tales discussed so far. It is also more directly concerned with open conflict. Yet its chief emphasis is on the inner turmoil of the boy in question—and in the resolution of that turmoil in a death of exquisite longing.

"The Outcast" tells how Uriel, a Hasidic rabbi, comes to a village one snowy Friday and is banished from the town by Avigdor, its rigidly sectarian *parnas* (burgomaster). The rabbi, as he leaves, curses his antagonist, saying that an outcast will arise from his seed. At just that time Reb (Mr.) Avigdor's daughter dies, leaving a brood of children. Gershom, the eldest, is a gifted Talmudic scholar and the apple of his grandfather's eye. And indeed, when Gershom comes home for the first Passover after his mother's death, he is overwhelmed by melancholy and goes by chance into a little Hasidic prayer house, where he finds both pleasure and release in the Hasidic service. He immediately rejects the experience, however, and reverts to his grandfather's Way, splitting hairs in his Talmudic studies, afflicting his body with ascetic exercises, and "encasing himself in sadness like a worm." His soul suffers, however, and craving the union he senses can come only through the medium of Hasidic exaltation, he sets out to find Reb Uriel.

A Hasid finds him fainting in the snow and brings him home. He recovers but languishes, until a mysterious stranger initiates him into the vision of ecstatic union with the deity that informs the Hasidic cult.

And since Gershom's heart was opened and came to glimpse the divine mystery within simple things, the stranger began to lead him from rung to rung on the ladder of wisdom. . . . At that moment the husk of that soul fell away, and all of Szibucz fell away from it. And such longings began to spring up in his heart as had never been known to the people of Szibucz, and they revealed themselves in his eyes, which labored in the Law and then sought to rise higher and higher, beyond. But his fingers were blind, and they groped in the world of truth as a blind man gropes in the darkness.[12]

As a result, "melancholy suffused him, and the anguish of the world veiled his pleasant face." Suffering, he moves further and further from the ordinary plane of rabbinic learning and human contact, "pouring out his soul, as a child into its mother's bosom," climbing and soaring into the "intelligible world" and striving to sit "in the shadow of the Holy One, blessed be He" and to "suckle from holy thought." But when the inspiration leaves him,

Gershom sits on the ground and puts his head between his knees like one who had been forced to alight from the chariot at the moment that the Holy Spirit went forth to greet its Father in Heaven. "My God, my God," Gershom cries, "you created Paradise and placed a sword at its gate. May it be your will that my bones burn in hell, if only a sixtieth part of them reach you in the end." . . . And a voice murmurs like a dove, "Alas, for the sons who were exiled from their Father's table." Exiled from Father's table, and when will they return? Has their time not yet come? The lowly world thou hast created— what remains for us within it? [13]

His final sense of release comes only when his master reveals the mysteries of the Song of Songs.

He had not yet finished when Gershom began to cry with all his might, "I will fly and wander far, and sing the Song of

Songs. To the house of the Lord we will go, we will go; we will tell the house of Jacob how my soul has thirsted, has yearned for the Lord." So he cried and cried, like a bird that has scented the fluttering of its wings, and flies, and murmurs as it flies.[14]

The scene then shifts:

The eastern sky reddens, and the dome of the sky nearest the earth grows dark. The daughters of Israel light their candles and stand in the gateway of their houses, murmuring to each other, "A good and a blessed Sabbath." As they wait, their chaste daughters come, with their hair dressed, in their lovely garments, and stand with them, facing the synagogues and the houses of study in order to be able to respond with "Amen, may His hallowed name be blessed." The householders, with their sons, walk to the houses of study and chant the Song of Songs, and the good Lord sinks the wheel of the sun in the west in order to receive his beloved, the Sabbath Queen, in chaste darkness.

At that moment Gershom entered the house of study and leaped onto the altar and lay his head between his hands for a moment. Then he lifted his head and began to read the Song of Songs with terrible ardor and awesome strength until he reached the verse, "Draw me after Thee, and we will run." And when he reached the verse, "Draw me after Thee, and we will run," his soul departed from his body, in its purity. His lips were still murmuring, "The King, he brought me into his chambers," when his soul expired with the words.[15]

Formally, "The Outcast" is concerned with the working out of a curse in the context of a conflict between Hasidim (ecstatic pietists) and Mitnagdim (legalistic literalists) at the time (the 1770's) Hasidism reached Galicia. The issues are crystallized in the representation of Avigdor, the rich, worldly, repressive pillar of the old dispensation with its emphasis on Law, and Uriel, with his melting, ecstatic cult of love.

Gershom's tragedy stems from the conflict in him between the way of the world, which is Avigdor's, and the way of transcendence, which is Uriel's. The story's main emphasis is on Gershom's anguish and the horror—mixed with ecstasy—of his doom. It is terrible that he should have to suffer; it is terrible that he must die, reaching into the world beyond for tenderness and love. It is also marvelous: a total transcendence, in feeling, of the limits of life in the vale of tears. In taking the mystic way, which he does not altogether choose, Gershom reaches out to his dead, beloved mother, as well as to God. The imagery of suckling at the breasts of thought, and of pouring out his soul "like a child into its mother's bosom," straddles the conventional metaphoric language of mystic communion and the concrete psychological realities of the boy's life. The tale evokes essentially the same ambiguity that informs Raphael's relation to the Torah scroll and the same reconcretization of metaphor that is achieved in "Agunot." So integral is Gershom's melting out of life at the end that it induces neither pity nor terror in the ordinary sense. Gershom wants it so badly and needs it so much, that the pity lies only in the fact that it took so long for it to happen, the terror in the fact that it is not really pitiable at all. And yet it is all very sad.

[6]

The balance of the feeling evoked in "The Outcast" is characteristic of all the tales I have discussed here—and of many of Agnon's other tales of *shtetl* life. They exploit the imagery of faith and transcendence, of union and communion as a way of conveying a sense of experience that at once laments mortality and celebrates the pain that it brings. One might say that "The Outcast" renders a characteristic moment and a characteristic mode of experience in the *shtetl* culture. But the emphasis is not on the substance of that culture or on the ancestral values that inform it. Rather, it is on the emotional values that arise within it, without reference to the validity of the problems or attitudes that give rise to them.

The most striking thing about the stories is the apparent objectivity of their form. One might say that Agnon does a triple take in rendering actions set in the ancestral world. First, he enters, though in a limited way, into the experience of particular characters who act and react within it. Second, he renders their actions and reactions much as *they* would have rendered them. And third, he casts the tale itself in a literary mode that would be congenial to the participants in its action. Reading such a tale, we apprehend the people, scenes, and events that fill the tale, but also participate in the attitudes and perspectives of those who act in them. Thus it is not only an action that we see imitated, but —implicitly—an entire mode of consciousness and a total vision of experience.

Agnon never attempts a discursive presentation of the grounds for and qualities of this vision. In fact, he never talks about the vision as such. Quite the contrary. The tales —again—are composed in the manner of folk tales. They employ a narrative voice that assumes we are tuned in upon its assumptions and can therefore focus directly on the things that concern it. The vision that animates the entire world of the tales is, in a manner of speaking, completely dissolved in their narrative mode.

Yet the depersonalization that the form of these tales involves should not conceal the extent to which Agnon uses them to project his most personal, his most intimate predilections. And these predilections are both complex and devious. The "modern" tales, written since the early thirties, suggest that Agnon turns to the ancestral world for the "wholeness" of experience it engendered. In tales both traditional and modern, moreover, Agnon suggests that the ancestral world is possessed of a power and a vitality which stun the imagination. One story—"The Fathers and the Sons"—presents us with a series of fathers, each older than the one preceding him, and each more fresh, more vigorous, and more vital.[16] The suggestion is that the narrator of that tale experiences a sense of impotence and insignificance in the face of the patriarchal world and the "fact" that the world is felt to deteriorate in power and glory with the passing of the generations. One presumes that Agnon resurrects the ancestral world to present us with images of that power and that glory.

Yet the power in question is a very peculiar one. It is, to be sure, the power to affirm life, but it is also the power to reconcile oneself utterly to life's negativity. The people and scenes depicted in these tales are always seen as diminutive—quaint, folksy, lovable. His people are, almost uniformly, little people with a quiet dignity. They are pious and prudent, deeply involved with the things that constitute their lives and remarkably gifted at letting go of them without crying havoc. Again and again we see them, in one of two perspectives. We see them experiencing pain and loss, not only stoically, but also with a kind of yearning pleasure. Or we see them comically abstracted from consciousness of the exigencies of ordinary life. In either case, there is beauty or amusement in their lives, but certainly not power or vitality in the ordinary meaning of the terms.

As a result, one has the sense that Agnon is performing a peculiar operation on the past which haunts him so persistently. If its grandeur lives in his imagination, that grandeur is cut down to size in the adulatory diminutives of his stories. It is as though he must shrink it to livable scale, not by directly challenging its existence or values, but by bringing it under aesthetic control. I often wonder whether Agnon's most pious evocations are not in fact voodoo exorcisms of a past that will not die.[17]

If Agnon is indeed resurrecting the past in order at once to celebrate it and to diminish (if not to denigrate) it, if he is in this way indeed circumventing a very real confrontation with decisive elements in his own experience, then a further quality of the tales takes on a striking significance. The tales of the traditional world rarely involve confrontation of the tensions to which their characters are subject or an exploration of the inner gounds of their conflicts. Just as "The Legend of the Scribe" renders the way fantasy and feeling are integrated within a prescribed pattern of relationships, so it renders the disintegration of that life—and feeling—pattern within rather formalized conventions of feeling and belief. It is surely no accident that Raphael, like Gershom, breathes out his soul in song. In these tales, song is the vehicle for the unquiet, the longing, the fear that the characters experience: it is Ben Uri's song that haunts

Dinah, for example. But song is also the medium of reconciliation and a final harmonization of discord, both for the characters in the stories and for their readers. That reconciliation comes in death. To expire is to breathe out the dying breath, and that breath is song, which both expresses the individual's craving for union and carries him toward the union he has craved.

The effect is peculiar. Agnon's finest noncomic work in the traditionalist mode has a kind of luminous loveliness and musicality, reminiscent of the medieval tale at its best. In it there is a fine orchestration of feelings that spring from pain and loss, but never a direct representation of the rawness and anguish they involve. Everything is harmonized within the dominant pattern of submission, and every discord is resolved within that pattern. The songs characters sing are one medium for expressing the feeling that there is a resolution. Another is the elaborate pattern of tropes from the repertory of traditional image and legend. But the final effect is somehow one of evasion. It is as though Agnon turns to the ancestral past partly because he finds within it a set of attitudes that permit a deeply desiderated transcendence of the harshness of inner conflict and a deeply felt need to circumvent the horror of death itself.

And that evasiveness leaves one uneasy. The stories have a quiet beauty. In sheer virtuosity there is little to match them in modern Hebrew letters. And they do, one feels, draw on something that was really present in the *shtetl* culture. Indeed, they do so with an authority and a compassion (despite the diminutives) that are moving. But the extraordinary aestheticizing of experience is suspect, as is the deep passivity they reflect. They are still more troubling when read in the light of Agnon's later work. There Agnon invokes dissonance. He renders characters who, like those in the earlier tales, yearn "beyond"—often back to the world of the earlier tales, that is, to the ancestral scene. And he projects, sometimes on a grand scale, the horror that informs such yearning in the modern world. Yet in the modern stories as well, however clearly the psychological and historical grounds of the dissonance are projected, one feels he is stepping away from the heart of the darkness— and illuminating it with an inadequate, aestheticizing light.

I am suggesting, in effect, that there is a much stronger affinity between Agnon's early, pathetic tales of *shtetl* life and his later, "modernist" work than at first meets the eye. There are stylistic affinities, of course, and there is the ever felt hand of the master craftsman at work. And there are the constant echoes of the classic Judaic idiom of faith. But beyond these formal and external elements there are the pervasive passivity, the recurrent "yearning beyond," and the constant craving for a wholeness unattainable in the present life.

One might see these qualities as the expression of a deep theological and existential intuition, of the awareness of man's deeply experienced sense of his vulnerability and violability, and of the only partial existence which is—at best—his in the flesh. One might hold that the melting sweetness and even ecstasy of the tales of the ancestral world evoke the way that the sense world is overcome by a tradition of faith, in which the felt presence of the deity creates the possibility of dealing with it satisfactorily. One might insist that the sense of loss and fragmentation of being that fills the modernist tales is the consequence of the characters' having been cut off both from the ancestral world and the deity who could be reached through the forms of life he prescribed.

But it seems to me that Agnon is writing about (or working with) something else: a deeply felt personal, one might even say infantile, sense of a wholeness that has nothing to do with the deity or his ways (unless one wishes simply to consider the religious feeling a direct projective of infantile needs). There is no question that he projects the sense of completeness with delicacy, mastery, and grace. But the struggle, the horror even, that ordinarily accompanies this craving for wholeness is never really there. There is no subversive resistance within the self to the felicities to which his characters consistently aspire.

Hence one comes away from the tales with a sense that something is lacking. It is impossible not to wonder whether the loveliness and musicality so worshipfully evoked are not, in the end, an evasion and a self-indulgence of Agnon's own wish to transcend the final terrors of mortality itself. Agnon, one notes, depicts pain, but never the pain of wayward inner resistance to striving toward objects of valid desire. And we rarely glimpse the larger, more dangerous impulses, which his people are generally and beneficently spared. When we do perceive them, as in Agnon's lyric evocation of a dreadful necrophiliac love, we perceive them in the glow of an aestheticizing so complete that it robs them of their life. Yet their luminous simplicity continues to beguile us.

[3]
The Bridal Canopy and the Comedy of Providence

Agnon's treatment of the East European village culture culminates in *The Bridal Canopy* (1931).[1] *The Bridal Canopy* is Agnon's first novel-length work. It is also the first to employ the complex irony that marks his later fiction. The earlier tales of the ancestral world lure us into the aura of a quiet pietism, but *The Bridal Canopy* forces us to stand at a considerable distance from it. *The Bridal Canopy* places its pious village protagonist in a deeply ironic light; it invites us to cackle at his absurdities even while it provisionally immerses us in his values.[2]

[1]

Reb Yudel, the protagonist, is an avowedly comic character in part identified with the scrawny cock who wakes him for his morning devotions. But he also embodies the faith that sustained the ancestral tradition. Through him, Agnon asks us to contemplate the quality of that faith and also to reflect on the conventional and factitious nature of faith itself. We are invited, moreover, to reflect, not only on Reb Yudel, but on the nature of tradition—any tradition.

In form, *The Bridal Canopy* is an elaborate frame story. Reb Yudel, an unworldly *batlan*—that is, a scholar who does not work for his bread—ventures into the Galician countryside to solicit a dowry for his daughters from the congregation of the faithful. In the course of his travels, he visits with a variety of people and hears a variety of tales. Virtually everyone he meets shares his pious point of view. Reb Yudel affirms the existence of a benign providence, and so do most of the people he meets. The action of the novel, moreover, seems to confirm his belief. Reb Yudel finds illustrious matches for his daughters, so that he comes to celebrate their nuptials at a stupendous feast, with virtually all the people he has met along the way present, listening to a wedding song that shows how virtue is rewarded and how the world is ultimately ordered by the Master of Ultimacies himself.

Yudel stands at the center of the action. Yudel not only travels in the world, but also reflects upon it. He is an inveterate ratiocinator, with a text—not always an altogether appropriate text—for every occasion and a need to expound the ways of the world and of the appearances that govern it. As a result, we not only see the world through which Yudel moves, but also enter into his responses to it. Thus *The Bridal Canopy* becomes a detailed study of a consciousness, the consciousness of a moderately individuated type who reflects the world view and psychic organization of the ancestral milieu as Agnon apprehends it.

The Bridal Canopy at once celebrates Reb Yudel and mocks him relentlessly. From beginning to end it provides us with a weirdly bifocal image of its hero, of his way of seeing the world, and of the world his way of seeing typifies. On the one hand, all of Yudel's presuppositions are confirmed; his faith in the government of God and the con-

gruity between the world and the Word seem to be borne
out by his daughters' marriage and his own "going up" to
the Land of Israel at the end. On the other hand, even as
we enjoy his successes, we are aware of the absurdity of his
relation to quotidian reality and of the precariousness of his
survival within it. We are also aware of the vision he embodies.

It is not that Agnon ever openly questions the bases of
Yudel's faith. His approach is far more subtle. The narrative tone of the novel is gentle and affectionate; it asks us to
participate in its protagonist's experience and vision, yet at
the same time the story parodies that vision. And the action
significantly juxtaposes Yudel's unrealistic attitude with the
hard realities of the world.

The confrontation between Yudel and the hard facts re-
sembles the confrontation between Don Quixote and his
world. Yudel has his Sancho Panza (an amiable drayman
called Nuta), Yudel goes on a rambling journey, and Yudel
has his pratfalls. Quixote embarks on his adventures without money or provisions, because knights-errant never
worry about such things. Similarly, Reb Yudel does not
duck when village boys throw stones, because he believes
in the efficacy of prayer. Yet Yudel later worries about
"bears, tigers, and snakes" in the forests of a Galicia, which
knows no such beasts, much as Quixote worries about sor-
cerers and goblins—as about chivalric courtesies—in seven-
teenth-century Spain.

There is a deeper affinity between Yudel and Quixote,
however. They share a radical, if sometimes sophistic, faith
in the literal applicability of a literary tradition to the circumstances of ordinary life. Yudel does not read romances,

but he does read the sacred texts, and he assumes that they apply to his ordinary experience. Yudel believes that the world is governed by God, whose intentions are revealed in the Word. The world can therefore be grasped, not by observing it, but by examining the sacred texts. If the world-as-observed contradicts the Word-as-revealed, one must somehow reconcile the two, by revising one's observation or by invoking more words to blur the discrepancy.

Like Cervantes, Agnon exposes the discrepancy between the world and the word, directing consistent—though gentle—irony against his protagonist. But his adventures end well for Yudel; his daughters marry and he becomes rich and goes to the Holy Land. Indeed, one should not labor the Quixote-Yudel parallel. Quixote enters an indifferent or hostile world, impelled only by his heroic illusion. Yudel enters a world that is wholly sympathetic to his aims; he ventures into it, not on his own whim, but armed with credentials provided by the sage rabbi of Apta. Quixote is drubbed by angry innkeepers; from the very first moment, Yudel is entertained by virtually everyone he meets. Quixote's "victory" is largely in the consciousness of the reader; Yudel's victory is tangible. He has lived in the spirit, but he triumphs in the flesh as well.

Yet the irony is there, in the story, constant and corrosive, contradicting his conception of the world. It figures from the outset in the tone of the narrative and the juxtapositions it entails. And it is sustained by a variety of devices which expose the contradictions that beset him throughout.

[2]

The contradictions in Yudel's situation are already evident in the novel's opening paragraph. Yudel, we are told, is a pious man who "worshiped the Lord in awe and reverence: His studies may be said to have been undertaken . . . not to do honor to him, or . . . to assure him a portion in the world to come. Rather, he sought to make of himself a seat for the Holy Spirit to dwell in"—though he lacks an adequate seat to sit on in the basement he shares with his wife and daughters. Yudel's entire existence is, in fact, devoted to transcending the things of this world—things his wife and daughters might involve him with. Abstracting himself from their dire poverty, he studies day and night, so that his soul may find itself "in the intelligible world, and be as if concealed from things of the senses." [3]

Yet Yudel's meditations comprehend the things of the world, even while they seem to negate them. Hungry after his morning prayers, "he would not rush home like a common worldling, to cram himself full of worthless and contemptible things, but would nourish his intellectual soul by contemplating the account of the manna in the Bible, and the like." Yudel, in short, avoids eating but uses his meditations to allay his hunger. Similarly, Yudel averts his eyes from matters of livelihood "and other such illusory things" but sets out to make the best possible match for his daughters. He negates the world in order the better to interpret it through the sacred texts, "manifest and mystic," but he nonetheless must exist in the world. And without real effort or reflection, he succeeds.[4]

Hence the most delicious irony of all: the fact that our pious protagonist, who averts his eyes from the world of "illusion," achieves the most worldly kind of success—and does so by conspiring, wittingly and unwittingly, to make the most worldly of worldly appearances. Yudel spurns appearances, but he agrees to pad his belly with a pillow, so that the people he visits will think him a prosperous man and therefore welcome him more heartily. And his journey is full of contretemps that stem from other deceptions: accidental deceptions, apparently untainted by conscious manipulation on Yudel's part.

How does Yudel finally accomplish his mission of finding a groom for his eldest daughter? By means of such deception. After traveling at random for months, he realizes he has raised two hundred gold pieces. Conscience-stricken at finding himself a beggar with such wealth in hand, he dismisses Nuta and settles at the nearest inn. There, setting aside worldly matters, he immerses himself in his sacred studies. Time passes. People, noticing him, assume he is rich. Who else sits—just sits—at an inn? He must be there on business. What business? Businessmen descend on him, but he pays them no heed: study is his only business. He must be rich as Croesus—or rather, Solomon!

By the time the innkeeper learns of Yudel's real mission, the local magnate is eager to make the match for his son. He is doubly eager when he learns Yudel's full name: Reb Yudel Nathanson of Brod—the name of a man renowned for wealth and charity. Is it Yudel's fault that he has the same name as the richest magnate in Brod? Or that no one calls him by his surname, so that it will be difficult to discover his real identity at the showdown? As for the fact that he agrees to match the twelve thousand gold pieces offered as the bride price—did not the sage rabbi of Apta tell him to pledge what the bridegroom would pledge? God, Yudel presumes, will help. Who is he to doubt the sage of Apta and God's bounty?

Indeed, why doubt it? At the crisis, his wife and daughters find a hidden treasure, which provides the dowry and more besides. Again we have evidence of the living charity of the living God. Yudel, self-effacing soul that he is, assumes that it is not his virtue, but rather virtue itself, that is rewarded by divine Providence.

Hidden treasure solves Yudel's problems and confirms his faith in benign Providence. Because there is so much good-humored participation in Yudel's experience throughout, we participate in his expression of faith as well. But we are also deeply aware of the conventional comic nature of the events that lead to the happy ending. For the action that intervenes between the formal engagement and the actual marriage involves an elaborate formal comedy of mistaken identities and a series of situations that underscore the fictive nature of the resolution. We are made to grasp the real illusoriness of the "world of illusion" in the course of a complicated comic sequence that employs a play within a play, a set of "real" and "illusory" Yudels, and the device —borrowed, like so much else, from *Don Quixote*—of having the "real" Reb Yudel pass into "fiction" as he becomes a legend in his lifetime.

The more immediate confusions have to do with the "real" Reb Yudel Nathanson, the magnate, who receives, at Purim time, the traditional bride gifts from the groom's family. Reb Yudel the magnate is childless, but his wife convinces him that he should not return the gifts—that he should play out the game in the hope of finding the bride and her father. Reb Yudel the magnate keeps the gifts, but he cannot find our Reb Yudel, who is known as Reb Yudel Hasid, and whom no one knows by his family name of Nathanson. Hence the comedy of errors at Purim, when our Reb Yudel visits Reb Yudel the magnate to seek alms for the poor. Since Purim is a time of traditional gift-giving and mummery, he finds at the house of Reb Yudel the Magnate a "Reb Yudel who is not Reb Yudel"—that is, a beggar who has been impersonating our Reb Yudel on the road—as well as a group of mummers who are representing his encounter at an inn with the very same "Reb Yudel who is not Reb Yudel." For Yudel has entered into folklore and has become a subject of popular representation.

By the laws of ordinary probability, this situation should have made for confusion worse confounded. But it does not. The encounter leads to nothing—nothing, that is, but our Reb Yudel's living through the pathos of his own journey as he watches the play, and a further realization by the reader of the conventions at work in the novel.

[3]

These conventions—that is, the conventions of comic disguise and comic contingency—operate first to drive Yudel toward catastrophe, and then to assure a happy ending. In doing so, they not only throw the contingencies of the world of experience into high relief, but also dramatize the contingent nature of Yudel's vision. At the same time, they serve Agnon's ironic purpose in creating the possibility of sparing Yudel the pain of experience itself. Yudel is invincibly innocent and invincibly ignorant of the world and its ways. As might be expected, this Yudel, cushioned in his pain-free existence, learns nothing in the course of his journey. Wisdom may be the reward of suffering, but Yudel does not suffer and therefore does not learn.

His lack of educability is also part of Agnon's ambivalent

joke. *The Bridal Canopy* is chock-full of precise historical and anthropological observation. It depicts a world that, however much the author helps us to overlook it, is full of poverty, suffering, and dangerous human quirkiness. We would, in the ordinary course of things, expect Yudel to undergo some sort of education. Indeed, we are told that he does learn: "From the travels Reb Yudel traveled, he arrived at a true perception of the world. On the face of it, this world we live in is not worth perceiving. But in view of the fact that he clarified his thoughts and drew the proper inferences from events, for him this world became a world of reality too." [5]

But what does Yudel learn? That there is nothing great or small in the world from which some moral or intellectual advantage cannot be garnered.

An ordinary person passes by a tanner's yard and holds his nose and flees. But Reb Yudel looks at the hides, contemplates them, and says, "If only I could flay the skin off my back and make scrolls of it, so that I could fulfill what is written in chapter 82 of the Book of Moral Chastisement: 'And I will chronicle all of my sins.' " [6]

In other words, Yudel learns only what fits into the structure of his own presuppositions—which means, again, that he learns nothing at all. As he contemplates the origins and sufferings of the Jews of Galicia, for example, he reflects:

I used to say, Why was [Galicia] called Galicia? Because in the beginning it was *galim v'tzia* [Hebrew for "ruin and waste —a phrase whose root consonants *gal* and *tzia* can be joined to make *galitzia*], but since I learned that when Titus exiled the

Jews, they came here, . . . I realized that they named it for *golei Tzion* [Hebrew for "the exiles of Zion"—again, *galitzia*, with a juggling of vowels], since the consonants coincide.[7]

It is not only Yudel who thinks in this way. The narrator goes on:

And we [that is, the readers, who, it is assumed, participate in his assumptions] would think so too, except that the stones of the place show that the Jews migrated long before that. For it has been found that some of the descendants of the Prophet Jonah are buried in the cemetery at Lemberg. Thus, we find a fish engraved on their gravestones, in memory of the fish that swallowed Jonah.[8]

And so on.

The crowning touch comes when Yudel gets back to Brod. He has "learned" much, and is pleased with what he has learned. But he puts it all aside "in order not to distinguish himself from other Jews in his learning." It is no accident, moreover, that "he lived with a handkerchief tied over his eyes for several years before he went up to the Holy Land." He is still committed to the "higher" vision of the "intelligible world," and does not wish to contaminate it by contemplating the lesser realities of the unintelligible one.[9]

[4]

The irony directed at Yudel is also directed against those who share his vision. A pogrom is averted because someone finds a cat. We are somehow asked to forget that the incipient pogrom was provoked by a Jewish burgomaster's irresponsible grief at the loss of that cat. The man who tells this story—and those who hear it—applauds divine Providence. Elsewhere, we hear how a poor man who has given his last penny to a suffering coreligionist is afraid to tell his wife about it. His wife, assuming he has lent the money at interest, takes on a "moneylender's look." Matchmakers, taking her for a rich woman, arrange advantageous matches for her daughters. Again, we are asked to applaud divine Providence: to affirm that it rewards the pauper for refusing to boast of his charity.

As with Yudel, so with the others who inhabit his world. Virtually all of them, so long as they work within the assumptions of their communal vision, "read" everything amiss. Hence, as with Don Quixote, but on a larger scale, the matter of motives—and of the appearances of the "word of illusion"—becomes central. Yudel does not see, cannot see, and at times does not choose to see the motives that underlie certain actions. The narrative, piling episode on episode and anecdote on anecdote, creates an elaborate contrapuntal play of appearance and interpretation of appearance, of illusion and counterillusion. The pattern is so complex that reality at moments seems just the play of unintelligible illusion that Yudel thinks it is. We are aware of the extent to which hard social realities are at work, and that no manipulation of them in anyone's consciousness can soften their contours. Hence we are amused by Yudel's incapacity to perceive them or deal with them. But we are also aware of the extent to which everything lends itself to interpretation according to his "system." We read things one way, Yudel another. Yudel's way is as coherent as ours —nay, more coherent. We think him funny as he makes his readings. He would think us mad for making ours.

So Agnon can at one and the same time undercut his protagonist and involve us in an action which, on the face of it, bears out all the presuppositions of his protagonist's vision. Yudel has his conventions of seeing, and the novel he is in has its conventions of action. Yudel's conventions of seeing prescribe happy endings because they affirm the benign nature of God's Creation. The novel demands happy endings because it is conceived according to the conventions of a kind of comedy that at once contradicts and confirms its protagonist's vision. Those conventions confirm his vision in that they demand a happy ending. They contradict it in that they stress social actualities, and are concerned primarily with worldly motives. Yudel's conventions coincide with the conventions of the novel he is in, not only in that they call for harmonization of the world which creates them, but also in that Yudel's otherworldly vision in no way negates the values and pleasures of life in this world. It is comic and incongruous, from our point of view, that the pious renouncer of the pleasures of the world should inherit all the goods of the world. But Yudel's tradition does not eschew the world. "Mine is the earth and the fullness thereof," saith the Lord, yet the world—with all its twistings and turnings—is meant for man. The ancestral tradition is, after all, an essentially this-worldly one.

Yet Agnon does everything in his power to make us aware of how conventional and contingent Yudel's organizing vision really is—as conventional and contingent as the conventions of this novel itself. The wedding feast at the end of the novel is climaxed by a song, an interminable but amusing narrative in doggerel which celebrates virtue and the harmony that is engendered by virtue. And it does so in

terms of births, marriages, and blessed settlements in the
Holy Land—that is, in terms that echo the terms of *The
Bridal Canopy's* own resolution. "The Song of the Alphabet" is a poem forty-two pages long, partly acrostic and
largely in the rough quatrains of the folk ballad. It tells of a
childless couple who teach the Torah to the children of Israel in times of trouble. Their struggle to educate the
young in the face of oppression leads the Alphabet to bless
them with many sons—as many sons as there are letters in
the Hebrew alphabet. The sons are named "alphabetically"
—the first Abraham, the second Baruch, the third Gedaliah,
and so on—and in their studies they are alphabetically
"matched" with the books of the Bible—Abraham studying
Job; Baruch, *Bereshit*—and later with the tractates of
Mishna and Talmud. Each, moreover, is alphabetically
matched with a secular science—Abraham with algebra,
Baruch with *balshanut* (philology). Each marries a girl
with an alphabetically matching name, and when the sons
finally follow their parents to the Holy Land, they settle in
places whose names alphabetically match their own—and
so on.[10]

If we accept, if only for a moment, the terms of this ballad, we see that the world is indeed as Yudel has always
held it to be: ordered not only in terms of the Word, but
even of the letters that make up the Word. The conventions of language, which are perhaps the most arbitrary of
conventions, come to be seen, not as arbitrary, but as mysti-
cally valid.

But like virtually everything else in the novel, "The
Song of the Alphabet" cuts two ways. It confirms the
"mystic" but rational order of creation, demonstrating the

conformity of "real" life to the "truth" of the letter; in doing this, it follows the kabbalistic notion that all truth is to be found in the *letters* of the Torah. At the same time, parodying this notion, it heightens our awareness of its precarious conventionality. It again highlights the extent to which Yudel's vision is contingent upon a set of conventions. At the novel's end, even as we "celebrate" Yudel's successes, we are aware that he is both saint and fool, and that his incessant intellectual and spiritual activity is at once vital and stultifying. It is vital in that it is perpetually self renewing, and stultifying in that it makes ordinary action in the ordinary world virtually impossible. But a further truth is that Yudel's existence is contingent on conventions that may seem arbitrary to us but constitute an absolute necessity for him and his world.

[5]

Our awareness that Reb Yudel's responses have their roots in a tradition of seeing and feeling is heightened by the elaboration of a literary theme akin to the literary theme in Don Quixote. Yudel not only derives his sense of reality from literature, but in the course of the novel he himself becomes the object of "literary" treatment, entering into song and story as a folk hero. About two-thirds of the way through the novel we learn that, with the return of Nuta to Brod, the Brod singers had begun to put Yudel's adventures into rhyme. And as Yudel wends his way homeward, we encounter the responses of his various hosts to the pictures drawn of them by the Brod songsters.

Thus, Paltiel, in whose house Yudel has spent the first night of his journey out, has heard the ditty on that visit even before Yudel stops in on the return journey. We hear that Paltiel's wife has been offended by it—it casts aspersions on her pancakes—as well as that Paltiel is pleased. And we finally hear the song itself, with its lame meters and vast simplifications:

> So the man of the house
> Thought it good time
> To spice their good talk
> With a draught of good wine

And he whisked out his wine
The best that one buys
To winnow one's thoughts
And render one wise

> And urged him his fellow
> To do him his will
> Who of the good draught
> Then quaffed him his fill

And the householder's wife
Dished up such delicious
Stuffed pancakes as nourish
All peoples Galicious

> And he feasted and frolicked
> For hours on end
> With pancakes for comfort
> And spirits for friend

Did our pious good Yudel
And his jolly good fellows
Till he suddenly felt
A pain in his bellows

> So he wept and he wailed
> Oh Paltiel, oh Sarah,
> Save me, oh save me
> From my gluttonous error
>
> So Sarah she boiled
> On her sizzling hot griddle
> A bag of hot water
> To put on his middle
>
> And what's more, the good Lord
> Afflicted Nuta his drayman
> With turbulent guts
> For ever and amen.[11]

The songs—like "The Song of the Alphabet"—are at once folksy, crude, and jolly—for example, the Brod minstrels' account of one Reb Kamtzi ("Mr. Tightfist"), to whose table some pranksters directed Reb Yudel:

> Pigeons' milk his daily draught
> Doughnut's hole his steady fare
> Haunch of roaches sauced and rare
> Grace his table, everywhere
>
> Shade of dungeon cuts he him
> In which to cloak his haggard skin
> Half a feather makes his couch
> He pillows in a flea's dark pouch
>
> Spendthrift, wastrel, Sir Skinflint
> He's the country's brightest boast
> Paunchy roaches he don't stint
> As ballast for his every toast.

And the children, we are told, would add:

Doughnut hole his daily fare
Dank dark shade for wear and tear
Paunchy roach he's sure to eat
At the foot of Judgment seat

He will gorge on roach's rump
At the sound of Doom's last trump.[12]

And so forth. Most of the main episodes of the journey out have passed into folklore by the time of the journey back. The songs are sung everywhere, and the chief episodes they recount are enacted in little plays the minstrels put on for popular amusement. Yudel must not only confront himself in song and story, but—in the hilarious denouement of the muddled-identities episode—must confront Reb Yudel the magnate in the presence of the sham, begging "Reb Yudel who is not Reb Yudel," as well as of the actor who is impersonating our Reb Yudel in the drama of his own "true" adventures presented on that occasion.

To be noted about this handling of Yudel's passing into legend and art is the fact that, just as Reb Yudel himself encounters the songs, ballads, and skits that have grown up around him, so we confront them and are forced, willynilly, to consider the discrepancies between the adventures in "works of art"—ballads, stories, or novels—and Reb Yudel's "real" adventures. We are aware that the folk romance of Yudel and his journeys constitutes a tradition of sorts. So we become aware of the simplifications, distortions, and complications that enter into the elaboration of any tradition—including the "true" revealed tradition according to which Reb Yudel lives.

We have, in effect, watched Yudel himself interpret his

inherited tradition in terms of the world he encounters, and the world he encounters in terms of his tradition. We have, moreover, seen the strange things the one does to the other in Reb Yudel's consciousness. Finally we see how Reb Yudel himself, in all his comic-pathetic peculiarity, has passed into tradition—a tradition of folk song and folk ballad that produces "The Song of the Alphabet," as well as the lame, comic Yudel ditties.

To cap it all, we have seen, much earlier in the novel, the way elements of the legendary tradition combine and permute in the mind and the mouth, not only of Reb Yudel, but also of Nuta—as when, at one point, Nuta is laid up with a bad back and spends his time telling the children of his hostess of his own adventures and those of their great-grandfather. In doing so, he fabulizes: Their ancestor grows rich, and his riches come from milk of a remarkable cow—a cow which, as we happen to know from an earlier episode, he never acquired. How does the cow's excellent milk enrich him? By curing the emperor of a dread disease. And where does Nuta get the idea of such a cure? As we happen to know, from an altogether different story Yudel has told him, a story having to do with the curative powers of citrons.

The literary theme pervades the novel. Even the minor episode of Nuta's legend-making is carefully "set" against a series of episodes specifically concerned with the transmission of scholarly writing—with how certain treatises came to be published (or not published) owing to their heretical or nonheretical contents; with how they were copied or not copied, destroyed or not destroyed, and so on. The theme is subtle but pervasive. It figures obliquely, for example in a story—already mentioned—about Lesunka, a cat. Lesunka's disappearance first causes, then miraculously averts a pogrom. It also allows the mice to consume valuable writings by scholars suspected of Sabbatean leanings.

I am suggesting that *The Bridal Canopy* is permeated by a consciousness of how precarious tradition itself is, as well as how tenacious. There is a pervasive sense in the novel of the contingency of Reb Yudel's tradition and, by extension, all tradition. There is also a pervasive awareness of how tradition shapes consciousness and is itself shaped by the encounter between the tradition-bearing consciousness and the reality within which it must subsist.

The awareness is augmented by the purely literary structure of the novel itself. In the telling of his story, Agnon manipulates his perspectives in such a way that we immerse ourselves in the make-believe world that he projects, even as we stand skeptically outside it. Insofar as we are outside it, we are aware of the imperatives of his literary convention, as well as of their arbitrariness. We are always aware, when on the outside, that it is Agnon, the teller of the tale, who is choosing to lead it toward its happy consummations, just as Reb Yudel, within the tale, is always choosing to read the world in his peculiar way. At the same time, we are aware that Agnon's apparently arbitrary methods in shaping his tale, and Yudel's in imposing his consciousness on his world, are necessitated by a set of incontrovertible determinants—Agnon's by the nature of the *literary* pattern he has chosen to work within, and Reb Yudel's by the unshakable prior assumptions of the tradition which he lives and interprets. Both are informed by the easy gaiety of the folk modes, in verse and prose, that Agnon invokes

—modes that override the lugubrious implications of much that the novel contains.

[6]

The Bridal Canopy is an extraordinary book, in its handling of both Yudel's world and Agnon's ambivalence toward that world. To begin with, it evokes the quality of thought, feeling, and judgment that informs Yudel's sensibility, and it does so on a heroic scale. Beyond that, it renders, as no other work does so extensively, the unique *shtetl* sense of nature and history. Much admired for this, it has been hailed as *the* "epic" of the old village culture, and as *the* representation of the *shtetl* before its decline. It cleaves assiduously to the particulars of Yudel's time, place, and idiom, yet there is nothing musty in its spirit. *The Bridal Canopy* breathes a kind of animation that explains the deep delight that its first readers—accustomed to denigration of the *shtetl* by a long line of reformers—felt on reading it.

Its achievement is heightened by Agnon's skill in conveying a sense of the underlying coherence of its world. Reb Yudel's world is a traditional world, marked by the continuity of its traditions. Its people have an awareness of the continuity of human types and relationships—an awareness that tends to neutralize the poignancy of time and change and to create a sense of a continuous present for those who participate in its modes. Again and again, *The Bridal Canopy* suggests the near-simultaneity of past and present in the legend-making imagination of the folk. It does so by conveying a sense, not only of universal participation in the literary tradition, but also of the near-identity of the people who tell the stories with the people who populate those stories. In the novel's traditionalistic world, people have no need sharply to distinguish themselves from their ancestors or from the prototypical characters of the tales that reflect their heritage. Hence, for all the profound historicity of the Judaic vision of the world, these people lack the poignant sense of time that we inherit from the Judaeo-Christian tradition.

The affirmative evocation of Yudel's world hinges, however, not on the traditionalist material that Agnon presents, but on the devices that heighten our awareness of the made quality of both the novel and the tradition it reflects. It is Agnon's reflection upon the nature of tradition that ultimately sustains his evocation of the tradition. This, of course, is the crowning irony of *The Bridal Canopy*, especially if the book is viewed in the context of Agnon's life and work. The very attitude that allows him to recreate the ancestral world of affirmations opens the way toward the nihilism that was increasingly to dominate his work. It seems that to see so clearly the factitious nature of tradition itself is to envision a condition in which tradition no longer can shape man's relation to himself, to others, to the universe. Yudel may be comic and fatuous in his blind faith, but his blind faith provides him with a ground on which to stand. Agnon's later heroes, equally ineffectual, as we shall observe, will lack the forms of awareness through which Yudel apprehends his world.

Hence—after the fact, at least—it seems no accident that *The Bridal Canopy* appeared at the same time as the first of the Kafkaesque tales that were later gathered in "The Book of Deeds." [13] The early thirties were, to be sure, a time of bewilderment for anyone who knew Germany well and who was deeply identified with East European Jewry. Agnon's tales of a nightmare world anticipate and reflect the Nazi era. But it seems to me that they also represent the exploration of a perception that must have crystallized in the writing of *The Bridal Canopy:* the perception of both the fragility and the functionality of a tradition like Yudel's. What this perception makes possible is the treatment of the isolated individual in the context of an eroding tradition—that is, the treatment of the situation that is at the dead center of Agnon's later work.

Earlier stories—such as "Nights" and "The Sand Dune" [14]—had rendered the experience of isolated individuals, full of longing and need. But these were usually heavily overwritten and they reeked with a stale romanticism. They involved poet figures by the seaside, with their dream maidens and moon visions. Agnon wrote them at the same time he was writing the tales of the ancestral world, and he made no effort to harmonize the styles or the interests involved. Only after *The Bridal Canopy* do the two modes begin to merge: in the tales of "The Book of Deeds," where eroticism and isolation are placed in the context of the lost tradition, and—in a very different form—in *A Simple Story* (1935), where the fairy-tale romanticism of the earlier stories is "set" in the realistic framework of a genre novel, concerned with the objective conditions of life in a family within a closely observed milieu.

I am suggesting that *The Bridal Canopy*, seemingly so monolithic and so steeped in the stable ancestral modes, presents a consolidating point for Agnon's most vexing perplexities. In it, far from naïvely evoking something that he loves and enjoys, he probes the cultural and metaphysical grounds of his tradition. In doing so, he opens the way to the harrowing vision of the modern world that unfolds in "The Book of Deeds" and in *Yesteryear*, his last completed novel, which reflects on the issues implied in "The Song of the Alphabet" and on the logical dilemmas of a "reality" which can be read as either comedy or providential guidance.

The Bridal Canopy seems pivotal in other ways as well. In it, Agnon finally expresses his ambivalence about the ancestral scene with an openness unprecedented in the earlier work. One can say that the tales of the ancestral world "diminutivize" the denizens of that world and substitute quaintness for vigor and active striving. But one can also acknowledge a gentleness and a tenderness, which one then insists are possible for Agnon only because his people are scaled down to a Lilliputian quaintness. In *The Bridal Canopy*, on the other hand, quaintness becomes almost grotesque comedy, and Reb Yudel, though treated with tolerance and affection, is blatantly a clown and a fool as well as a saint and a scholar. It is as though still another condition for evoking the ancestral world on an "epic" scale is the ability to see it as laughable. It is, so to speak, possible to love Daddy only after one has cut him down to size.

One notes within the novel, moreover, an intensification of the characteristic Agnonic ambiguity in assessing values. Yudel is great, and Yudel is foolish; Yudel is God's fool, and Yudel is a scrawny cock; Yudel is Yudel, but Yudel is also someone else. The method of this novel is rooted in its bifocal vision, which makes us at once accept and reject the reality it presents. Such doubleness of vision will be still more operative in later works.[15] In *A Simple Story* one is already hard put to tell which way the ironies go. In a later novel, *A Guest for the Night* (1939), one has trouble distinguishing the Guest's illusions from the realities he affirms: Is his Palestine the real Palestine or the imagined one? Which is Agnon asking us to relate to? Agnon does not quite tell us; one feels he does not quite know.

Indeed, one suspects that the great value of bifocal vision or double perspective or rich fields of ambiguity lies in the freedom it gives him to sidestep the crucial act of judgment and the choices judgment entails. Paradoxically, after *The Bridal Canopy*, Agnon went on to perform heroic feats in evoking the milieus he has observed: the novels that follow confront—within limits—the twentieth-century world as Agnon has known it. Yet even as he presents these worlds, he comes to rely ever more heavily on the obscurantism of his method, which permits a blending of fantasy and reality, and a generation of symbols so ambiguous that their meaning eludes us. Agnon's movement into the fully contemporary scene takes place under cover of a technique that spares him confrontations of the most radical sort—a technique forged in *The Bridal Canopy* in evoking the ancestral world, which is not the ancestral world as it really was, but a fanciful version of that world as alembicated in Agnon's imagination.

[4]
Backwater, Buczacz:
The World of Agnon's Youth

Agnon pokes fun at Reb Yudel. He reduces the ancestral folk to a Lilliputian quaintness. But he endows them with a quiet charm and treats them with a touching (if ambivalent) reverence. There is, however, little to alleviate the harshness of his response to the world he knew as a youth. Writing of turn-of-the-century Buczacz, he confronts a culture for which he feels profound contempt, though he seems unable to shed an invincible (if ambivalent) sympathy for some of its victims.

[1]

The breakdown of Yudel's world and Yudel's vision dominates Agnon's turn-of-the-century work. In "Young and Old Together" (1923) and *A Simple Story* (1935) he renders a scene in which the old pieties linger on but have deteriorated into hidebound pietism or empty conformity.[1] We see how the old pieties no longer define individual lives, even though no new modes of self-definition have emerged. One culture has broken down, and no other has taken its place. Even the quality of protest, among those vigorous enough to protest, seems absurd. And human suffering, though pitiable, seems fatuous.

The depiction of external historical change is simple.

The study house and the ritual bath are no longer the center of communal and familial life. Middle-class people send their sons to secular *Gymnasia* and employ tutors to educate their daughters. Instead of congregating in the synagogue, young men dawdle in Zionist clubrooms, read the newspapers, and muddle over the problems of political life. Older people are utterly absorbed in their businesses; the ritual order figures only as a backdrop for their commercial and familial activities. Communal activity is undertaken conspicuously, with a view to enhancing one's social position.

The shift in manners reflects deep-seated political, social, and economic changes. Galicia was part of the Austro-Hungarian Empire, where an enlightened regime had progressively enfranchised its Jews and included them in the life of the larger community. In a period of expanding trade, moreover, Galicia had become one of the breadbaskets of Europe. Produce was exported not only to Vienna, but to Germany as well. And Jews played an active part in that expansion.[2]

Under the old order, the Jews, as a wholly discrete minority, had operated from a ground of radical, communal otherness; now they functioned as a minority with a measure of at least theoretical parity. For the most part, to be sure, they remained clearly identifiable as Jews and continued to suffer various handicaps and persecutions. But the identity of the individual Jew was no longer wholly defined by his origins. Up to a point, at least, an individual Jew could deal with a Gentile as merchant with merchant, if not as man with man.

The consequence, at one level, was a deep erosion of the

traditional patterns. Jews felt more at home in their environment. They no longer conceived of themselves wholly within the old, self-contained system of transcendent sanctions. Reb Yudel's consciousness is largely immersed in the communal consciousness. We recognize him as an individual, but the norms of his life and vision are clear, self-consistent, and communal. Yudel does not call himself into being by pitting himself against the world. For Yudel, the active, perceiving self is more or less given. So are its norms and its world, where things must be perceived and distinctions made. That world is a relatively static world, within which people have relatively fixed places and values.

The inhabitants of the Buczacz of circa 1905 lack Yudel's a priori certainties. In their world, "The Song of the Alphabet" is no longer sung; there is no total ordering of reality within the given conventions of seeing and being. Each individual must forge an identity with which to perceive the world and his place within it. Each, moreover, must choose among various modes of seeing and being; each must act effectively upon a relatively fluid world if he is to find a place at all.

These circumstances could have made for greater openness and a sense of the possibility of individual and communal development. Agnon suggests the opposite. He sees the subversion of the old order and the impact of that subversion on the individual. And he feels contempt for the objects that the "freer" people of Buczacz pursue and for the sensibility that hankers after such objects.

One sure ground for his contempt is the blindness of Jewish burgher and worker alike to a seemingly ineradicable anti-Semitism. Neither economic progress nor political enfranchisement had effectively overcome the prevailing antipathy, especially among the Slavic population of Eastern Galicia. There may, on the whole, have been little immediate danger to life and limb, but the long-term threat to security was real, and the prevailing complacency therefore ominous.

What to *do* about the problem was a matter of sharp controversy. Some Jews argued for socialist revolution. Some favored Zionist renewal. Some accommodated themselves to the established order, swallowing their pride and toadying to their oppressors. The majority merely lived out their lives, relatively oblivious of the future.

Agnon does not labor the political and cultural issues, though they are carefully worked into the fabric of his fiction and contribute to the grotesqueness of the town, as he renders it. What engages him, essentially, is the psychology and characterology of the Buczacz community, as it responds (or fails to respond) to the internal and external stimuli that impinge upon it. His judgments are made in terms of the quality of his people as people—as feeling, dreaming, active human beings. And the judgment at which he finally arrives is worked out, not only in terms of the community's ongoing life, but against the background of the ancestral world and its values. The emergent social scene is rendered in fine detail, but Yudel's world continues to provide touchstones for judging human values.

Agnon had rendered the ancestral world in relatively static terms. Within it, action and passion were almost wholly bound up with the old forms of spiritual striving. From within our own more or less Faustian sense of life, the people in Yudel's ambience seem to exist in a state of lulled activity; they submit to "fate" and rarely strive to master their environment. Yet they always convey a sense of meaningful struggle within their fixed patterns of existence.

In the tales that render the scene of Agnon's youth, on the other hand, there is a substantial intensification of activity. Political enfranchisement and commercial expansion have provoked vigorous, far-flung involvements. Yet there is a striking diminution of the sense of purpose, meaning, and choice. Agnon seems to prefer the ancestral passivity, which acquiesces in the given conditions of life and consciousness. But in turn-of-the-century Buczacz passivity has another meaning. There are restlessness and acquisitiveness; there is the will to assert oneself and to satisfy desire; there is the conscious will to change the conditions of existence. Yet one has the impression that the activity is not action but motion—mere motion, denoting moral and spiritual stagnation.

For Agnon sees the world of his youth as a stagnant backwater which is the more hideous because of the vain egotism that animates it. As he presents it, it is essentially the normative world of late-nineteenth-century fiction. Buczacz is not unlike Flaubert's Yonville de l'Abbaye, but it is often more horrible. Its inhabitants are more homuncular than Flaubert's Homais and more stilted and self-seeking than the ambitious small fry of Chekhov's plays. If personality and individuality are emergent possibilities in turn-of-the-century Buczacz, their exponents lack—at least as Agnon presents them—the dynamism that might make them viable. There is no one in the world of these tales who has the energy, the passion, or the potentiality for self-awareness that could bring him into vivid existence.

The curious thing about Agnon's treatment of the Buczacz of circa 1905 is the fact that he does not side with the contemporary individual any more than he sides with contemporary society. His sympathy is rather with the old communal consciousness: a consciousness that could shape the individual for its ends and use him for its purposes.

The quality of his characterizations is always a fair index to his sympathies. The tales of the old *shtetl* emulated the traditional modes of folk tale and homily. They rendered character in stylized, almost stereotypic ways. Yet their characters, however simplified, always had a felt roundness and a sense of subjective richness. The tales of turn-of-the-century Buczacz, on the other hand, employ the conventions of modern fiction. They have affinities with the work of Flaubert and Gogol, Chekhov and Gottfried Keller, Sigrid Undset and Turgenev. Their people have a more diversified experience than Reb Yudel, and we learn more about their public and private selves. Yet they seem flatter and less substantial than Reb Yudel and his peers. Even Hershel Hurwitz, the protagonist of *A Simple Story*, seems shallow and pallid by comparison, despite the considerable complexity of his characterization.

The flatness of such people reflects a judgment, and a devastating one at that. For Agnon their flatness is obviously a measure of the debility which has overtaken the ancestral world. This judgment, as qualified by other, more elusive responses, is the ground on which Agnon builds the fiction that is concerned with turn-of-the-century Buczacz.

[2]

"Young and Old Together" (1923) is a mordant satire. Its target is the shallowness of Buczacz in 1907 and its lack of organic relation to either a vital past or a meaningful future. Deliberately flat in characterization and ramshackle in structure, the novella touches on a wide range of motifs that were to be developed in Agnon's later work: the debasement of tradition, the adulteration of language, the disintegration of community, the deathliness of naked self-interest, and so on. Its judgments are devastating. All of them are implied in the name the novella uses for Buczacz and in the book's title.

Buczacz is an old Slavic place name. Agnon refers to the town by this name in the tales of the ancestral world. Here he calls it Szibucz (*shibush*), a Hebrew word denoting a blurred, muddled, or debased condition. The title, in turn, is derived from a rousing poetic call to action by Y. L. Gordon, the Hebrew Enlightenment poet, who challenged the Jews to leave Europe after the pogroms of 1881. Gordon's poem was popular at the turn of the century, expressing the urgent will to transvalue Jewish values and transform Jewish destiny. Agnon uses it here in a wholly ironic way, to comment on the community's crippling incapacity for meaningful action.

The novella's plot is brutally ironic as well. It opens as a group of young Zionists, defeated in the 1907 Austrian elections, see their candidate off to Vienna. Hearing a rumor that there is a pogrom in the nearby village of Pitshiritz, they rush to "save" their brethren. They see no sign of violence, however, so they gorge at an eating house, visit local Zionists, and arrange for them to have a nationalist "evening" at a later date. On their way home, however, the visitors are accosted by Alexander, a young anarchist worker, whom they think contemptible, but who intervenes on their behalf when some drunken Gentiles accost them. Alexander, who has been exiled from Russia for revolutionary activity, is arrested; the Szibucz gallants merely wolf down another meal and go home.

Things have been happening in Szibucz too. Gold has challenged Silver to a duel for insulting a Mrs. Silverman at a lecture. Hemdat, the narrator, tries to intervene, but the storm blows over without him. Gold wins Silver's girl and inscribes him in the "Golden Book" of the Jewish National Fund.

Hemdat has his own troubles. His grandfather, who is of the old school, takes him to task because he does not pursue his sacred studies, and his father asks him where he is headed. Hemdat himself is afraid that Alexander will be deported to Siberia. He tries to get the Jewish burgomaster to act on Alexander's behalf but succeeds only in eliciting sympathetic blather—and ends up watching the burgomaster extort a lavish dinner from an innkeeper.

Hemdat may well worry about the bankruptcy of the political and cultural ideals to which he is committed. Yet his grandfather's traditions seem as thoroughly eroded. Going back to Pitshiritz for the Zionist evening, Hemdat calls on the rabbi—who he knows has purchased his pulpit —and finds him shoving the "funny papers" under his Talmud. Noting that the rabbi's windows have been broken by vigilante pietists, he observes that sectarian schism has caused more damage than pogroms.

Finally, as his train pulls out of the Pitshiritz station, Hemdat sees Alexander in chains, probably about to be deported to Russia. His sense of the pathos and absurdity of the situation is heightened by knowledge that Alexander's fiancée, Sheine Pessel, who aborted during the "pogrom," has been impregnated by Deixel, the leader of the Zionist faction, and that Deixel is utterly impervious to the moral or human implications of the seduction or its consequences.

Alexander is the human pivot of the tale. We see him wholly from without, through the eyes of a sentimental prig, and we therefore can have no direct experience of him. Yet his generous manliness—whether real or sentimentalized by Hemdat—is the measure of everyone else's emasculation. Alexander, Sheine Pessel, and Reb Pesach, her father—these are the true victims of the reality in which everyone in the novella lives. They seem to be almost the only feeling, suffering people in the tale, and hence the only real ones. Yet no one will acknowledge either their reality or the reality that destroys them. People live in terms of stilted public modes of discourse or action, modes that serve merely as vehicles for private vanities, or are caught up in the pettiness of their most immediate concerns.

Ostensibly, it is around the public world that the novella's action develops. "Young and Old Together" is set against the background of the Austrian parliamentary elections of 1907—the first in which Jews enjoyed full electoral rights. The elections had stirred the community, especially its Zionist members. Since the founding of the Zionist organization by Theodore Herzl in 1898, the latter had turned their backs on local politics. But Herzl's death and his failure to get a charter from the sultan of Turkey had dashed their messianic hopes and revived their interest in local affairs. Hence the profound sense of disillusionment when they realized the elections had been rigged against them.

Objectively, to be sure, the elections precipitated only a minor crisis in the consciousness of the town. They served at most to underscore the community's equivocal relation to its neighbors and the precariousness of the future it was hoped the elections would secure. Agnon's concern, however, is not so much with the elections themselves as with the town's moral climate at the time. That climate is revealed in the course of the events—the journey to Pitshiritz, the skirmish with the drunken Gentiles, the arrest of Alexander, and so forth—which unfold in the wake of the elections. It is a poisonous climate, and one that seems the more deadly because no one is really aware of its painful ambiguities.

The shallowness of the prevailing consciousness is revealed most tellingly through Hemdat, who tells the story in the first person. Hemdat feels superior to almost everyone and everything, but he has almost no distance on himself or on the milieu he is rendering. He is one of the valiant band of Zionist youths on whom the action centers—young men of eighteen and more who are enrolled in the university and fill their time with politics and tattle. A generation earlier, they would have occupied pews in the study house and—as married men—filled places at their father-in-laws' tables. But they have loosed their bonds with the past, though they have no point of vital engagement with the present, nor any articulate image of the future.

Hemdat seems to be distinguished from his fellows only in being in some ways still more callow than they. He does, in the course of the action, seem to undergo a kind of confrontation with his triviality and theirs—but even that is minimal. He tells of awful things, but always in a tone of half-reverential bewilderment; if there are rumblings in his consciousness, they are subterranean indeed.

Hemdat's tone is full of preening sentimentality and priggish self-congratulation. "Young and Old Together" opens as follows:

Dr. David Davidson Leaves Town, and We Go to See Him Off

The train stopped at the station. Passengers peered out of the windows. Two or three people rushed ahead and were swallowed by the smoke. The locomotive lingered a while before leaving, and we stood by, to honor our candidate, Dr. David Davidson, on his departure. Dr. David Davidson, our candidate, was going home to Vienna, and we, the Young Zionists of Szibucz, had escorted him to the train.

How we loved him and his lectures! How we loved the cast of his features and his conversation! He even spoke Yiddish. He even went to synagogue the Saturday before the elections. Confound those who said it was done dishonestly, to win the hearts of the Jews, so they would vote for him—who said he had lived in Vienna for years and never gone to pray. It never occurred to them that he had done it out of love—love of the people he had chosen to choose him in the elections. There are doctors in this world who write books in praise of the Torah and its commandments even though they don't observe all the commandments in the Torah. It's not the deed that matters, but the light of a Jewish heart.[3]

Hemdat is obviously an innocent, with nothing but hollow sentiment and even hollower sentimentality to sustain him. The story twists and turns; unpleasant things happen; and much of what happens registers with him. Yet his essential tone does not change. We end up in a railway station, with a point of great significance to be driven home —and this is what we get:

I said goodbye to . . . all my Pitshiritz friends. Mr. Deixel helped me . . . up the stairs of the train, and all the Zionists in Pitshiritz stood there and cried, "Goodbye, goodbye, goodbye."

There is still one more drop of ink at the tip of my pen. As I stood at the window looking out, I saw Alexander with iron chains on his hands, [with] an armed policeman leading him. I don't know if . . . they were taking him to . . . the provincial capital or were deporting him to Russia. I told Mr. Deixel what was on my mind. . . . Mr. Deixel stuck his nose into the circlet of flowers he was carrying and sniffed them. Then he affectionately put his hand on my shoulder and said, "Right. There is no complete joy here in the Diaspora." The chains were old. They were rusty, and red as blood. The policeman seemed to be squeezing Alexander's hands so hard that his blood ran down the chains. But Mr. Deixel's flowers were fresh and fragrant.[4]

The speaker's nonjudgmental flatness and rhetorical primping are essential to the devastating effect of the story as a whole. That effect hinges on the tension between Hemdat's misplaced affect and the legitimate emphases of the action itself. Yet the flatness of "Young and Old Together" is felt to be a function of the flatness of the reality it renders as much as of the sensibility that renders it. Though we are irritated by Hemdat, we feel that there is no other way of treating this reality.

Everything contributes to the effect. The people in the story are Dickensian or Gogolian caricatures, whose names are congruous with the flatness of their presentation: Mundspiel (Mouthplay), Oberschenkel (Upperthigh), Chasirmeirinski (Piginpokeman), Sweintuchinski (Swineinasson), Calabinski (Dogson) and Buchav'cherpinski (Shamefitzscandal). Last but not least, there is Mr. Aniv'afsi'od (Iamyselfalone), a poetaster who has learned "all the languages of Europe" from dictionaries and is currently translating the regulations of the local burial society into archaic German.

These people are flat, vain, self-important. Their qualities, however, bespeak more than a merely idiosyncratic dimensionlessness. "Young and Old Together" conveys the sense of a shadow world, populated by human shades who, in their selfish idiocy, have betrayed every possible value. They travesty not only the old standards of *shtetl* decorum, but, insofar as they have them, their own, self-posited ideals; they are as much out of touch with their personal futures as with the communal past. Amusing themselves at cabarets where vulgar actresses impersonate Hasidic boys, and talking to anti-Semitic Gentiles who parody the parodies of Hasidic songs these actresses sing, Hemdat's friends also parody their own "progressive" ideals.

Those who wish to regenerate the community wish to regenerate themselves as well. Yet they are tangled in such idiocies as planning duels over imputed insults to fatuous clubwomen. The dueling motif itself involves a delectable irony. Szibucz' interest in dueling is in abject emulation of the imperial capital. But it can also be taken to be a parody of the Nietzschean will to manliness. But the conditions of the duel, like the fact that it never takes place, make manliness a grotesque and irrelevant quality. The grotesqueness of the episode is underscored by the juxtaposition of Hemdat and his friends with Alexander, who is a man and who bears the brunt of everyone's emasculation.

The betrayal of the past is as pointed as the betrayal of the future. The former is elaborately pilloried in the episodes involving Hemdat's grandfather. His grandfather takes him to task for abandoning the traditional texts as prime objects of his concern and goes on to lament the fact that prosperity does not make for commitment or value. "In the past," he says, "we used to study in the synagogue, six or seven lads to a single tattered text, by the light of a dim candle."

But the world didn't dim upon us. I would be satisfied if at the moment of my death I might feel even a sixtieth part of the sweetness I felt in my youth. But now, praise be, all the houses of study are filled with beautiful books, and every book is brilliantly printed—and here you go and abandon their study.[5]

Books play a central part in the story. They figure in the presentation of the Pitshiritz rabbi and in the choices Hemdat must make. They figure more vividly in a grotesque sequence in which a peddler of mousetraps sells a newfangled mousetrap to Hemdat's grandfather. The grandfather is vexed because mice have been gnawing at certain of Hemdat's books—undesirable, "enlightened" books, to be sure, but books nonetheless. When challenged about his willingness to acquire an untried device for dealing with vermin, he answers, "Fashion against fashion, fad against fad. Against mice that have fed on fashionable [i.e., modern and enlightened] books, one can use nothing but fashionable weapons." And Hemdat agrees with him, noting that he had once had a secular book bound with a sacred one, and that the mice had gnawed the one and spared the other. Even rodents, Hemdat implies, distinguish between the sacred and the profane, as humans do not. Yet, while the peddler is hawking his wares, we hear a housewife tell how mice had devoured her marriage contract—a religious document—and on the Sabbath at that.

The mouse-and-mousetrap motif is central to the tale and frequent in Agnon's work. For it not only evokes a sense of the grotesque mutability of values but bears upon the problem, so focal for Agnon, of transmitting the tradition. It figures in *The Bridal Canopy*, in connection with manuscripts gnawed to bits while the cat Lesunka was away. And it figures in some of the modernist works, to signify the destruction and desecration of the tradition and the immediacy of unhallowed instinctual desire.

More closely attuned to the question of contemporary Buczacz and its relation to its past, however, is another sequence, touching on both marriage and violence. At one point, Hemdat runs into a Mr. Hoffman, who is a descendant of Kraindel Charney, Menashe Haim's long-suffering wife in "The Crooked Made Straight." Together they meet Isaac Mondspiel. Mondspiel has been visiting his young wife, who left him because he was not as rich as she had thought. Asked whether she will come back, Mondspiel replies: "Why should she? She has a good job; she has admirers; she is taken horseback-riding and to libraries." Hoffman is shocked, observing that "one puts Hannukah candles in one's windows, but keeps one's wife in one's house."

Then Mondspiel indicates that he has brought Hoffman's little son a toy gun as a gift for Lag Ba'omer, the festival on which Jewish children traditionally went into the fields with bows and arrows to play at being Zealots and Romans —that is, to emulate the heroic Jewish resistance to Roman tyranny at the time of the Second Temple. The child, however, takes another tack.

[He] strapped his weapon to his thigh and strutted about like a soldier, terrorizing the household with his shots and his shouts:

> I am Teshil, the big, strong cop.
> I smack, I smash, I beat the Jews up.
> I shoot, I shoot: pop, pop, pop.
> I'm the boss, I run the show;
> The Jew he cries, O, O, O.
> I am the boss, the boss am I;
> The Jew he cries, Ai, Ai, Ai.

Yitzhak Mondspiel slapped Velveli on the back and said, "What a man, what a man!" Mrs. Hoffman took her son in her arms and proudly kissed him on the lips. Mr. Hoffman nodded and muttered, "New ideals! Teshil the cop! What grownups hardly dare to think, the children shout from the housetops. Every generation and its ideals! I can remember a man who trounced his son for slacking in his zeal for studies, who warned him that if he didn't study, he would end up like so-and-so—so-and-so being a famous general!" [6]

The Velveli episode serves to dramatize how far Szibucz has come. More than that, it captures the way people drift unselfconsciously. Indeed, throughout the novella, lack of self-consciousness seems still more dreadful than deliberate hypocrisy, of which there is no dearth. People are so self-involved and so unaware of themselves that communication is virtually impossible. Every effort at communication between characters betrays a vagarious irrelevance to the real issues. The dialogue that Hemdat reports is almost static; speech and gesture rarely "go" anywhere; they have the quality of slow, frozen motion in gelid space. People speak, but never to each other or to the point; again and again we have monologue, internal or external, directed to a vague object. No one gets whatever point is, with or without express intention, being made.

This is so pronounced that neither speakers nor listeners seem to have any real inwardness. People speak "in character" and are always clearly and consistently themselves. But they lack real subjectivity, and they are not clearly aware of each other. There is, to be sure, a field of discourse, rich in affect and poor in subjective meaning, common in varying degrees to all the Jews in the novella—a field of communal reference, both religious and historical, which survives in the community, though it has already been eroded among the young men who constitute Hemdat's circle.

Even where it survives, however, it is being progressively drained of significance, if significance is measured in terms of relevance to the ongoing concerns of the people. How people speak reveals who they are, but the idiom in which the characters speak is a parody of communication; insofar as it is the idiom of the old faith, it merely reveals how far they have drifted from its real basis and content. The public world in which Yudel once participated is parodied by the public world of para-Zionist Szibucz or proto-Orthodox Pitshiritz. That parody, as much as anything else, signifies its end.

[3]

A *Simple Story* (1935) renders the same phenomena, but in a different perspective. It centers, not primarily on the manners of the *shtetl* in transition, but on the inner experience of a young man unwittingly in conflict with both himself and his environment. It is essentially a study of repression, madness, and final adjustment within the bourgeois family, as we know it from turn-of-the-century European fiction. Perhaps Agnon's most fully resolved novel—in purely novelistic terms, that is—it renders the hopelessness of burgher life in Buczacz by juxtaposing it with the older *shtetl* on the one hand and the world of romantic fantasy on the other.[7]

In its fable, *A Simple Story* is very simple indeed. Hershel Hurwitz, sixteen, is drawn to Blumah Nacht, an orphaned cousin who works as a servant in his parents' house. Manipulated by his mother, he marries Minah Zimlich, a rich farmer's daughter. Hershel is unhappy and resentful. After Minah conceives, he goes mad and is sent to a sanitarium, where a kindly doctor sings to him, chats with him, and restores him to sanity. By the time his second child arrives, his life is like that of all the petty burghers of the town. He can no longer even recall the grounds of his former unhappiness.

The *story* is simple enough, but the *novel* is almost *too* rich in complication of plot, method, and—at times—substance. *A Simple Story* seems to start out as a romantic tale of young lovers who are thwarted by their elders—in the mode, say, of "Agunot." But it moves toward neither of its predictable endings. That is, it presses neither toward tragic devastation nor toward a comic resolution in which the will of the obstructive elders is overcome. Rather, it moves toward an ironic reconciliation of the hero with those elders and their values. Yet, though Hershel is treated ironically, we are somehow relieved when he "makes it" in conventional terms and "becomes a man." We end by partially approving a reconciliation to a milieu which has been shown to be inimical to every value of youth, life, love, or, for that matter, authentic tradition. Still, we go on scoffing at that milieu.

Hershel's reconciliation is achieved, moreover, in the course of an action that involves virtually no open conflict. Hershel is an ineffectual blob, unable to assert himself on any ground, and his mother is too cunning to challenge him openly. Even Hershel's true-love longings involve a radical dependence: he is drawn to Blumah's well-baked cakes and, when the crisis comes, is angry at *her* for not having taken the initiative, for having failed to act to thwart his mother. Though his vanity is tickled by his having been made a man through marriage, he cannot even follow through by playing his part adequately or by adapting it to the needs it stirs in him. Madness is his only form of self-assertion. His crippling rage can express itself only when, essentially emasculated, he crows like a cock and croaks like a frog. This phase passes, however, and without active effort on his part.

Furthermore, Hershel is as incapable of self-consciousness as he is of choice or action. Altogether, he is an impossible hero for a novel of sentiment. Yet, working with and through him, Agnon constructs a novel of muted power and deep sensibility. He does so by working the tension between the amorphous night world of Hershel's feelings and the harshly lit actualities of his daytime existence. In this, *A Simple Story* is reminiscent of *Madame Bovary*, especially in the way it establishes Hershel's inner life as at once the mirror and the antithesis of his environment.

Hershel's case, to be sure, is in many ways more dire than Emma's, and the modes of its representation are sometimes more complex. Limp and enervated, Hershel is capable neither of the articulate expression of rage nor of the demented energy that finally destroys Emma. Yet, as with Emma, we feel he has potentialities that cannot flow in the channels assigned to them by convention. We sense, moreover, a world of emotions pulsing somewhere beyond the painted flats of his immediate environment. Such emotions, though they may be obliquely intimated, cannot find embodied expression anywhere in Hershel's world. They are shallow and often factitious, yet their denial is felt to be terrible. This is why we can at once be reconciled to Hershel's reconciliation to his world—and be outraged by it.

As in *Madame Bovary*, the inner action unfolds within a finely articulated social setting. We see the prosperous Hurwitz household, with the shop downstairs and the dust-covered parlor upstairs, with Mrs. Hurwitz dominating both. We see the flourishing Zimlich farm, with its amplitude—and its anxieties. We visit the salon run by Minah's parvenu boarding-school friend. And we contemplate the pathetic pretensions of the establishment in which Hershel is stranded with his stick of a bride.

Beyond the circle of burgher households, we see the Zionist reading room where Hershel dawdles, and hear of the socialist reading room, where one Dr. Knabenhut struggles to improve the conditions of the working class; we meet

Getzel Stein, a clerk in the Hurwitz shop, who vainly aspires to Blumah's hand; we hear how Getzel's father fights for a franchise as a ritual slaughterer; we glimpse the grinding poverty of the Stein household. And so on.

Agnon vividly renders a circumscribed world that is undergoing a sea change in the slow time of provincial boredom. The egg market for Germany opens up, so that Szibucz prospers, and people complain about the price of eggs; shop clerks unionize, and Mrs. Hurwitz grumbles; Mr. Hurwitz donates paint to refurbish the old synagogue, and there is murmuring about the old decorations. Altogether, it is a world of expanding trade and eroding traditions. The old synagogue decor *is* painted over; the daughter of a pious milkman turned farmer goes to boarding school; young men peruse the newspapers, not the sacred texts.

In depicting this milieu, Agnon evokes the quality of feeling that informs the life of its people. He suggests a painful tamping of affect; it is inevitable that entire stretches of the novel have the broad caricatural quality of "Young and Old Together." At the same time, the world of *A Simple Story* is suffused with a prosy lyricism, somewhat reminiscent of the atmosphere of a Chekhov play. People send out tendrils of desire, reaching furtively for more satisfaction than they have, yet anxiously clutching at what they possess. We are always aware of the hopelessness of their desire. We are often aware of its aching triviality. We even know its gross and pathological sources. Yet we somehow—if only partially—are led to sympathize with it.

Hershel, of course, is the chief embodiment of such desire. In his love for Blumah, he is always drifting off into "worlds" of romance; when he comes back to the "world of reason"—that is, of good sense and cash registers—he is, we are told, "as one drugged," who has "taken a sleeping potion and then returned." Blumah, too, drifts off into "worlds of freedom" as she sits on the Sabbath eve, lost in her novel. Agnon does not specify the content of either Hershel's or Blumah's reveries. Blumah withdraws from the scene of the action when she learns of Hershel's engagement; after that we only glimpse her as a gray-garbed figure, chastely resolute in adversity. Hershel, on the other hand, remains in full view. But as he sinks ever deeper into depression and madness, he seems more and more to lack positive expectation and becomes more and more opaque to himself and his family. Again, we have no immediate knowledge of the content of his reverie; we enter only into its mood.

This is not to say that we get no insight into the content and nature of his desires. Quite the contrary. Without for a moment resorting to the language of the clinic, Agnon provides a full-blown clinical portrait of his protagonist. We see Hershel's mother as a cold, self-seeking woman who gives little but caters to her own pleasures (chiefly gustatory) and asserts her own will. Ambivalently, Hershel hates her but is unable to assert himself against her. Blumah, who is her antitype, attracts him at first with the cakes she bakes. This is significant: she is a mother figure—an idealized being toward whom he directs his repressed longings, but also his repressed animosity. It is toward his wife, however, that his deepest rage is directed before—in his madness—it is turned on himself. Asleep at Minah's side and fearfully stirred by desire, he dreams of slaughtered cocks.

As he goes mad, he wishes that all the cocks in the world might be destroyed. It is no surprise that he crows like a cock in his madness and loses the power of speech.

The clinical pattern of his cringing passivity is emphasized by what we are told of his "cure." Dr. Langsam speaks to him of his own village and sings him songs he heard in childhood from the lips of blind beggars in the market place. These are "soothing melodies that have no beginning and no end, so that your heart melts within you as you hear." They have a powerful healing effect:

The doctor's voice had already grown old and raspy, but still the sweet sadness would well up in his throat and envelop Hershel like a lullaby, such a lullaby as Hershel had never heard in his cradle. Ziril, his mother, knew her voice was unlovely and therefore did not sing to him as mothers do, and the *agunah* [deserted wife] who was their servant then—she was either occupied with household matters, or she was busy sewing herself a shroud, and therefore did not sing.[8]

Presumably, exposure to these songs releases Hershel from lifelong bondage to his rage against an unloving mother. After his release he has access to positive desire; he comes not only to accept his circumstances but to enjoy his wife, even to crave paternity. His bond with life, moreover, puts him in touch with death: "At no time," we are told, "was Hershel so aware of death as he was at that time." This too passes, however. One day, as he walks in the snow with Minah, they hear a blind beggar singing a "song that has no beginning and no end." For a moment, they stand, rapt. Then Hershel lurches away and throws a coin to the blind musician. After that, we hear nothing of music, beggars, or Langsam. It is as though, having undergone his therapy, Hershel cuts himself off from conscious relationship to the means of his rehabilitation—and to the deeper, more distressing stirrings of his nature.

The clinical pattern is clear, but it does not exhaust the content of Hershel's "disease" and its cure. Dr. Langsam's blind beggars, and the range of their associations, intimate a realm of transcendent experience. They point to noumenal reality: to a realm of being, not becoming; to paradisal satisfactions; to the exquisite reality of death. Presumably, it is the world which their melody symbolizes that Hershel longs for in his adolescent reveries, reveries touched off by his feeling for Blumah. Indeed, only within that enchanted world can Blumah be the fairy princess he apparently feels her to be, and Minah the mermaid daughter of a king.

Agnon regards that world ambivalently, however. There is a long history of madness in Hershel's family: an ancestor put phylacteries on his cat, and his mother's brother went mad and ate grass in the woods. Fearing madness, Hershel remembers them; trying to rationalize his own condition, he intermittently romanticizes them. They are anything but romantic, however—indeed, they are almost a judgment on his house—and if the melody has anything to do with them, we feel, it must be destructive.

Much the same is true of the romance quality that intrudes on the consciousness of various characters in the novel. For they find romance in the presence of village maidens and the strains of the songs they sing. We apprehend these strains in snatches, as characters immersed in their drab daily routines become aware of "something beyond." That something, as reflected in the sexual desirability of the maidens and the magic of their songs, is full of charm and enchantment; it also carries the threat of extinction. Under the influence of such song, Minah becomes for Hershel "a king's daughter with the skin of a fish"—that is, both an enchanting mermaid and a castrating horror.[9]

One is tempted to take such an image in a wholly clinical way: as the record, in poetic terms, of Hershel's anxious, unconscious response to his wife. And indeed, it is largely through such images that the pattern of Hershel's psychic life is revealed. Yet they also have another effect. There remains, beyond the clinical suggestion, a sense that the feeling symbolized by dance, music, and fairy tale has a completely autonomous, irreducible reality and value of its own. It does not merely serve as an ironic commentary on the constricted world of Szibucz or as a medium for psychic revelation. Rather, it points to a mode of feeling and being that is potentially accessible to everyone, and is arbitrarily excluded from Hershel's world.

Art, for example, would seem to give access to such experience. Hershel rejects the blind beggar who sings in the snow, and after a period of unaccountable joy and inexplicable grief he remembers that "Minah had learned how to play the piano, but . . . had never asked him for a piano to play. Like all men who have no feeling for music, he was grateful to his wife that she refrained from deafening his ears." [10] There seems to be a link between the hostility to music and the rejection of the blind musician, who seems to symbolize the exquisite intensities of both love and fate.

It is from the vantage point of such sensed possibilities that Hershel's final adjustment seems bleakly problematical. There is no doubt that, given his character, he is better off in the end. But his adjustment is achieved at the price of every possibility for growth or experience. As he dandles his second son, he seems aware that the price of his happiness is Blumah's continued loneliness and the misery of his first child, an enervated stick of a boy who was conceived in hate and so neglected at the time of his father's breakdown that he becomes a virtual idiot. Thoughts about such things seem to flit through his mind at the end, but they seem to be accompanied by the negative injunction, "Don't think about it!" [11]

Such advice seems prudent. To think would be to madden. The forward motion of life demands sacrifice and the tolerance of sacrifice. Hershel has let Blumah go, and he has renounced every impulse that might draw him toward her—that is, that might thwart and enrage him again. It is suggested that in doing so, he has given up, not only access to the noumenal realm by which all vital experience is fed, but an aspect of his soul as well. For Blumah, whose name means "night flower" as well as "blocked" or "blanked" night, may be seen as the feminine, dreaming aspect of his soul, akin in function to the moonstruck dream women of "Betrothed" and "Ido and Enam."

For better or worse, Hershel leaves that aspect of his being behind him for the sake of his place in the world. It seems good that he does so, since access to other modes of being means madness for him—as it has presumably meant madness for all the ancestors whose insanities have constituted a kind of curse on the house. Indeed, Agnon's treatment of Hershel underscores the shallowness of his conscious involvements and the vulgarity of the patterns into which his fancy falls. Though his needs are deeply rooted, his fantasies are hardly more than enactments of textbook romances. It is more difficult to imagine Hershel acting constructively to fulfill his dreams than it is to think of Emma Bovary doing so.

What remains for him seems rather dreadful, however: a life akin to his parents' life. Their essential experience is rendered in a little countinghouse idyl, halfway through the novel.

The door is half shut but the till is open. Baruch Meier and Ziril are sorting their money, copper here, silver there, bills elsewhere. They stack the coins and then they roll them, and tie the bills in packets.

Nothing is more pleasant than to sit in your store in the evening with your money stacked in front of you. You lay coin to coin on the table and somehow feel you have managed to get where you wanted to go. Couples stroll outside and, as they pass your door, they splash each other with mud. If you have ears in your head, you can surmise how their hearts feel from the way their feet plod. Alas! How many evenings have they wearied themselves thus, and how many evenings will they still go on wearying themselves so. I don't know what good will come of it all. And all the time you sit with Ziril your wife in your store, and the smell of figs and raisins and cinnamon rises in your nostrils. The shadow of the shadow of another sun inhabits that fruit. Even if it sits in its box, you can feel its warmth. Ziril and Baruch Meier sit together as one, their ears cocked. What have they heard that they cock their ears? Perhaps it is an echo of the songs the workers in the vineyard are singing or the echo of a kiss a shepherd gives his betrothed in the shade of a fig tree—perhaps it is this they have heard, and cocked an ear.[12]

This is the pattern Hershel has accepted. Baruch Meier, who jilted Blumah's mother to marry Ziril, the boss's daughter, has shut night, nature, and the power of Eros out of his life. He has abandoned himself to the claustral proprieties of the cashbox and the buffet. His domestication seems complete. Yet it is clear that "other," inappropriate kinds of feeling intrude on him and that he must deliberately negate them as he struggles to keep them out.

Essentially, this is the world in which Hershel finds his place. He may have greater access to feeling than his father had; his therapy—and indirectly, his madness—may have created the possibility for a richer relationship to his wife. But his world now defines the limits of his feeling. It is clear that he can (and will) no longer reach beyond the scope of the given.

The structure of issues here is closely akin to that of Thomas Mann's *Buddenbrooks*. There, too, we see how the burgher life involves repression of "real" desire. There, too, we see how desire, sent underground, wells up in maddening forms. And there, too, we see the deathliness that is harbored in negated life energies. The essential difference lies in Mann's humanist suggestion that the chthonic strains of disruption can, ideally, be sublimated in art and that a richer awareness of the issues might permit their subsumption within an ordered existence. For Mann the tension is always there, but the possibility of transcending it is, even within the terms of the Schopenhauerian pessimism that pervades the novel, at least conceivable.

For Agnon, on the other hand, the acute tension seems a product of the specific historical circumstances that are rendered in *A Simple Story*. In those circumstances, there seems to be no way of reconciliation to the remote music, unless it is through complete withdrawal from the life of the times —as in the experience of Tirzah and Akaviah Mazal, the protagonists of "In the Flower of Her Youth," who also figure in *A Simple Story*, as the couple with whom Blumah Nacht finds a home in the end.[13] For there is nothing in the social world that would validate a commitment to it— not even the compulsive energy that informs the life of bourgeois Lübeck, as Mann presents it. And, though art, in the abstract, *might* afford a mode of integration, we are made to feel that no art adequate to the task could arise in Hershel's milieu—that is, in Szibucz of 1907.

[4]

A Simple Story is as vigorous as "Young and Old Together" in etching the mores of Buczacz of 1907, and ultimately as harsh in judging their human implications. Where it differs from the earlier tale is in its readiness to enter into the intimate experience of its people, and in doing so to complicate both our perception and our judgment of them. However we judge Baruch Meier in his countinghouse, we participate in his responses to the night sounds outside. However we question the depth or viability of Hershel's feeling for Blumah, we participate in the quality of his longing. Indeed, the aesthetic texture of the novel, with its delicate patterning of nervous, lyric responsiveness, implicates us in the immediacies of the feeling-life of all the people in it.

It is owing to the empathic involvement that *A Simple Story* becomes the moving but baffling novel it is. In it, Agnon again works in a mimetic yet parodic mode analogous to the one he employed in *The Bridal Canopy* and the tales of the ancestral world. He not only tells an intimate and sentiment-laden story, but he tells it in the accents appropriate to its milieu. *A Simple Story* is not only about turn-of-the-century Buczacz; it is also the kind of story that might have been written for turn-of-the-century Buczacz—for people of Hershel's background at least. It is told in the tone and idiom of his class.

At the same time, it ruthlessly parodies that tone. The narrative voice of the novel is constantly invoking the rigors and mercies of "God in Heaven" in a way that can only undercut any faith in His relevance to the ongoing business of life. The speaker of *A Simple Story*—that is, its narrative voice—is vaguely pietistic, and sentimental. The strength of his storytelling lies in his capacity for moment-to-moment empathy with the characters his narrative seems to mock. But he lacks the fine discrimination and distance that his narrative requires; he finally participates in the vulgarities which are native to the milieu he seems—at one level—to pillory. Agnon's irony is directed as much against him as against the burgher world of the novel.

As a result, the very tone and idiom of the narrative voice reflect the debasement of the old traditions. Such a debasement is explicitly manifest in the representation of the novel's world: in the mindlessness of the Hurwitz' wish that Hershel be a rabbinic scholar, in the apathy of Hershel's own drifting from the study house to the Zionist reading room to the marriage bed, in the glazed idiocy of his involvement in Zionist politics and thought. But as in "Young and Old Together," the narrative tone in a sense becomes the final indictment of the debased order. It suggests the clouding of intelligence and sensibility at the most intimate level of judgment and sympathy; indeed, the narrative tone, with its carefully manipulated ironies, echoes the aimless sentiments that characterize the world of the novel as a whole. The ideas of God, providence, moral economy, and the like have become clichés, counters of consciousness that lack fixed meaning or reference in the historical world. So have the more radical sentiments of its people. "Young and Old Together" excoriates the emergent turn-of-the-century sensibility for its insensibilities. It suggests an absence of Eros as well as an absence of legitimate objects for Eros. *A Simple Story* makes a more telling indictment. It engages sentiment and sensibility at the most intimate level; it suggests, not an absence of desire, but an absence of legitimate objects of desire and of legitimate forms of experience within which to satisfy desire.

Agnon's response to the spiritual condition he depicts in the novel is more complex than his mockery of the narrative voice would suggest. Its complexity is revealed in the handling of his protagonist. Young men madden often in the work of Agnon's contemporaries: Y. H. Brenner, M. Y. Berdichevsky, U. N. Gnessin. The madness, symbolic of the communal corruption, ordinarily springs from conscious alienation or revolt. Brenner, for one, sought out the most self-conscious types in his milieu and subjected them to the strains of a typical experience. Agnon, on the other hand, chooses a type with minimal self-awareness. Hershel has virtually no self-awareness, being essentially as remote from it as Georg Büchner's Woyzek or Eugene O'Neill's Yank. He is, moreover as grossly manipulated by heredity and environment as any of Zola's protagonists. Incapable of struggling against his environment, he is incapable of serving as an instrument for revealing the unexplored possibilities of that environment. He can only suggest the limitations it imposes.

Yet, even while mocking him ruthlessly, Agnon often

participates uncritically in his feeling-life. One senses that he writes about him out of a deep affinity. At the same time, he seems compelled to reject him, even as he rejects the state of mind to which he adjusts: the state of mind, that is, which is pilloried in the narrative voice. We have the same depth of ambivalence here that we have seen in Agnon's relation to Reb Yudel, though the terms of the ambivalence are different. Yudel is idealized and then mocked; Hershel starts out contemptible, yet there is a sympathy for him that the mockery would not lead us to expect.

Essentially, of course, Hershel is like the protagonists of all of Agnon's longer fiction. His bumbling incompetence, his lack of effective will, his repressed aggression are characteristic of Reb Yudel, as well as of the Guest and Yitzhak Kummer, who figure in the later novels. Agnon has the gift of taking a human type—a kindred human type—and of shaping him to fit the circumstances of the historical moment he seeks to chronicle. Moreover, part of his pleasure in historical recapitulation—what has been called his "epic" endeavor—seems to lie in casting such a type, with his limited range of conflicts, into various historical circumstances. His very passivity allows Agnon to make him a vehicle for a historically conditioned pattern of responses—the responses that were probably dominant in his time.

Several ends are served by Hershel's helplessness. First, Agnon uses his passivity to convey a sense of the fate that pursued young men in his culture. Second, through him he explores some of the roots of his protagonists' prototypical passivity. That is, he intimates the relationship between radical repression of hostility and the ineffectuality that dogs his characters—an insight that he will elaborate in the treatment of Yitzhak Kummer in *Yesteryear*.

Third, he finally brings into clear focus one of the central preoccupations of his work: the impact of coercive, regressive, unembodiable desire. He had touched on it in the tales of the ancestral world, in such stories as "The Legend of the Scribe." There, however, desire is ordered according to the terms of the ancestral tradition and its sense of transcendent objects. Here, in the absence of legitimizing forms and ends, desire can only unnerve and unman. In later work, where the more conventional novelistic framework is abandoned, we see it—as in "Betrothed" and "Ido and Enam"—working itself out with a compulsiveness that ends in ecstasy and death.

Thus *A Simple Story* is a kind of halfway house in Agnon's development. In it, the problem of dislocated desire casts off the traditionalistic and folkloristic trappings of the ancestral tales. It should not, moreover, seem surprising that here, in depicting the world in which he himself came to consciousness, Agnon finally touches on a situation so close to what one takes to be his own deepest concern: the need to celebrate insatiable desire. And he cannot negate desire itself.[14] At the same time, he seems unable to imagine an exponent of desire more positive than a Hershel. Nor can he, it seems, see any reason to: his Hershel is a faithful reflector of the milieu he is representing. There seems to be no ground of transcendence in Hershel's relation to his world.

As a result, Agnon presents a highly static portrait of a culture and of an individual, in which all the artistic elements seem integral, but in which none of the *issues* are resolved. If *A Simple Story* has a fault, it is identical with its greatest strength: the extraordinary aestheticizing of experience, so that every word, every gesture, every vignette has the kind of beauty we associate with genre work of the impressionists and the postimpressionists. Agnon has caught the hopelessness and the longing of people in Hershel's milieu in the fixative of a detached and mocking art whose substance is a subversive sympathy for every nuance of that longing. In doing this—here, in his most conventional piece of fiction—he achieves the kind of horrified empathy with the commonplace that energizes the work of Joyce and, still more glaringly, of Beckett, in which the flat commonplaces of the prosiest sensibilities are evoked with love and delicacy only to assure us of the idiocy of their experience —and ours.

This balance cannot be sustained. The ancestral world calls for both affirmations and negations that diminish Agnon's ironic distance. Reb Yudel must be first cut down to size and then celebrated in ways that make for artistic complications of the sort discussed in the preceding chapter. The modern world, on the other hand, elicits a degree of revulsion that leaves little ground for empathy with anyone except the typical Agnonic protagonist. As a result, the modernist tales differ from *A Simple Story* almost as much as *A Simple Story* differed from the tales of the ancestral world. Clearly, what served to render Hershel's world—the blancing of a genre rendering of milieu against a lyric evocation of the substrata of consciousness within it—will not do for the more ravaged modern scene. A starker, more angular mode of storytelling will have to be created to capture the discontinuities of action and the hauntings of consciousness that typify the experience of modern man as Agnon sees him.

Yet, though both style and narrative mode change, the

balance of feelings toward the passive Agnonic hero remains fairly constant. Agnon may see his later heroes as
more pitiable and more contemptible than Hershel, but the
painful ambivalence remains: the adherence to his protagonist's modes of feeling and desire on the one hand, and
the cruel mockery of his feelings and desires on the other.
There also remains the painful inability to resolve the ambivalence. The result is another kind of muscle-bound fiction,
agitated by the drift of fantasy and the flickering of desire,
but never touched by the immediacies of thought and feeling as we know them.

[5]

Between the Then and the Now:
A Guest for the Night

A Simple Story depicts the *shtetl* in decline, *A Guest for the Night* its ultimate decay.[1] Agnon's last novel of *shtetl* life, *A Guest for the Night*, published in 1939, reads like a prelude to the Holocaust. Focusing on neither past glory nor impending doom, it evokes the bewilderment that overtakes a man who reaches for a past that he cannot forget or restore. As it registers what that man sees and feels, it chronicles the erosion of the village culture and the extinction of its human types.

[1]

Historically, *A Guest for the Night* reflects what happened to the *shtetl* in the decade following World War I. *Young and Old Together* and *A Simple Story* had rendered a process of inner decay, stressing the secularization of an essentially religious culture and the impact on consciousness of a modicum of political and economic freedom. *A Guest for the Night,* on the other hand, probes the condition that follows from the disruption of all social, political, economic, and religious institutions. In the background of the experience it presents are the conquest and evacuation of Galicia by Polish, Russian, German, and Austrian armies in World War I; the disintegration of the

Austro-Hungarian Empire in the aftermath of the war; the pogroms of the postwar years; the mass emigration; and the progressive decay, under the impact of war, famine, pogrom, and persecution, of the moral and spiritual life.

All of this is refracted through the experience of the Guest of the title. The Guest is a nameless native of Buczacz-Szibucz, a man who emigrated to Palestine in his youth and who returns for a visit in the middle of his life. Burned out of his house in Jerusalem and temporarily separated from his wife and children, he means to be "but as a guest for the night." Instead, he tarries for a year. The novel itself is his first-person account of that tarrying and the confrontations it brings. These not only induce a deepening consciousness of the doom that has overtaken his village, but also lead to a reassessment of the dreams that have animated his own life.

The Guest is full of muted longing. What he seeks is not a particular Proustian encounter or the reinstitution of a particular set of relationships, but rather the sense and tang of the past, as that past lives on in memory. He craves the scent of "millet boiled in honey" that prevails in "the town from the day after Passover to the end of November." What he finds is a desolate community and a ruined town. He describes what he sees as he walks from the train station after his arrival:

Of the large houses of two, three, or four storeys, nothing was left except the site. Even the King's well, from which Sobieski, King of Poland, had drunk when he returned victorious from war, had its steps broken, its commemorative tablet cracked; the golden letters of his name were faded, and sprouted mosses red as blood, as if the Angel of Death had wiped his knife on them. There were no boys and girls standing on streetcorners, there was no singing, no laughter; and the well spouted water, pouring it into the street, as water is poured in the neighborhood of the dying. Every place was changed—even the spaces between the houses. Nothing was as I had seen it when I was little, nor as it had been shown to me in a dream shortly before my return. But the odor of Szibucz had not yet evaporated—the odor of millet boiled in honey, which never leaves the town from the day after Passover to the end of November, when the snow falls, covering all.[2]

The home place has been devastated by the Great War and by the afflictions that followed. Most of its Jews have fled or died; the handful who remain have returned only after much wandering. These are racked by poverty and consumed by the physical and spiritual afflictions of the times. All vital institutions having collapsed; the returnees lead a kind of post-mortem life.

[2]

The world the narrator enters is full of the insulted, the injured, and the maimed. His train is flagged down by a one-armed war veteran with a rubber prosthesis. He is shown to his hotel by Daniel Bach, whose wooden leg replaces the one he lost while earning "a Jewish livelihood." Throughout his stay, he is shadowed by Ignatz, a foundling with "a Jewish mother and a Gentile father, or a Gentile father and a Jewish mother," whose nose has been shot off in the war, and who walks around, begging, with "three holes in his face." When the Guest needs a coat, he goes to a tailor whose wife is an asthmatic who hopes she can be cured by smoking grasses of her native place. His mother's nurse, now an old woman, has lost six of her seven children. She dies when the seventh is away, so there is no one to close her eyes in death. Reb Chaim, a one-time Talmudic prodigy, lives alone, penitentially hewing wood and drawing water.

Still more telling is the prevailing sterility. No child has been born in years. The one child we observe closely is a thirteen-year-old cripple, too weak to leave his bed, and weirdly clairvoyant. Another set of children are the spawn of a half-literate carter who freezes to death in the snow. Raphael, the cripple, cannot walk; the children of Hanoch, the carter, cannot read and are therefore beyond the pale of the tradition.

The tradition itself is in a state of advanced decay. Many people still go to the synagogue, but most of them are cynical and demoralized. Those who believe do not always pray, and those who pray do not necessarily believe. The children of the Guest's innkeeper tend to mock the rituals and traditions; the innkeeper himself, though he observes the rituals, does not go to synagogue, because of his rheumatism. Bemused, he sits with his eyes half closed. "I don't know," the Guest wonders, "whether to recall what has passed or to avoid seeing what is still to come."

The innkeeper's family reflects the ravages of the recent past and suggests the desolation to come. One son is an effeminate fellow who is having an affair with a rather masculine, married Polish lady; another is a cardsharper; the third child, a daughter, is a flapper who carries on with a traveling salesman. All three children mock every form of religious and familial decorum. A fourth child—Rachel—is a graceful girl, who reminds the Guest of the "princeliness" of the children of Israel. She marries Yerucham Freeman, a lapsed Zionist, who has turned Communist, a man who assiduously builds roads in an effort to rehabilitate the town. Yerucham's roads either lead nowhere or to the cemetery.

The novel is a mosaic of the Guest's encounters with a variety of such types and of meditations upon such encounters. The external action is negligible. The Guest must find a place to stay; he finds one. He needs an overcoat; he has one made. He is given the key to the old study house; he loses it and has another made; he goes back to Palestine and leaves the duplicate key as a gift for a newborn babe. While in Szibucz, he haunts the study house and immerses himself in its lore. In winter, he assembles a small congregation around his fire, only to lose it when spring comes at last. In midwinter, he is implicated in the disappearance of Hanoch, the half-literate drayman who brought him wood to stoke his fire. He gets involved with Reb Chaim, a one-time scholar, who stokes the study-house fire for him after Hanoch's death. He visits with Rachel and Yerucham, who confronts him with the thoughtlessness of his enthusiasm for Eretz Yisrael (the Land of Israel) in his youth. Finally he goes home to Jerusalem.

The external action is marked by brief stretches of low-keyed narrative tension. The real action is inward, unfolding in the Guest's consciousness as he confronts the town and becomes aware of his expectations about it. This process of confrontation is also fragmented, however; but it is cumulative, and is ordered chiefly according to the pattern of the seasons and in terms of the symbolism of the ritual year, as these rhythms press upon the Guest's growing self-awareness.

And the movement of the action is complex, counterposing intricate patterns of birth and death within the cycle of the seasons. In the course of his stay, the narrator sees the last relics of the old order die, but he also celebrates the birth of a child in the town. That child is born to Rachel and Yerucham, with whom he feels a real affinity, despite a deep rift in ideology and judgment. An upward swing, coinciding with summer and birth, is heightened by the Guest's return to Palestine. On returning, he visits Daniel Bach's father, a pious old man who has emigrated from Szibucz to the Holy Land and become deeply involved in the agricultural life of his settlement. The old man's attitude stirs the hope that the original key to the house of study, which the Guest finds in his suitcase on returning home to Palestine, will one day be of use to him—when, in accordance with an old Midrash legend, all the prayer houses and study houses of the Diaspora are transported to Palestine.

But this hope cannot obliterate the Guest's awareness of the utter debilitation of Szibucz and its traditions. The Guest immediately perceives staggering external changes in his Diaspora village. He apprehends the cripples, the dead silence, the ruins. But the inner—the spiritual—lack is also directly evident when he enters the synagogue on the eve of Atonement, immediately after his arrival.

There was not a man I knew in the synagogue. Most of the worshippers were recent arrivals, who occupied the honorable places by the eastern wall and left the others empty. Some of them had risen and were walking about, either to show their proprietorship or because they did not feel comfortable in their places. The radiance that is wont to shine on the heads of the sacred congregation on the Eve of Atonement did not shine on their heads, and their prayer shawls shed no light. In the past, when everyone would come to pray, and each would bring a candle in addition to those that burned in the candelabra, the synagogue was brightly lit, but now that the candelabra had been plundered in the war and not all came to pray, the candles were few and the light was scanty. In the past, when the prayer shawls were adorned with collars of silver, the light used to gleam from them upon the heads of the worshippers, but now that the adornments had been carried off the light was diminished.[3]

The Guest soon grasps the immediate sources of the debility. He hears about years of wandering and war, of poverty and pogrom—of how women and children wandered in alien cities, while husbands and fathers suffered death and mutilation on the battlefield. He compares the old days, with their thriving trade, to the present, in which freezing old women offer rotten nuts and apples to nonexistent customers.

[3]

The Guest's awareness of the objective reasons for poverty in the present grows side by side with his heightened consciousness of the decay that had begun to mark the life of the town in the past—a decay he himself had fled in pursuing the Zionist dream. Invited to speak to some Zionists, he tells them about the prewar Zionist and socialist reading rooms, with their fly-specked newspapers, their desultory chitchat, and a membership in quest of a cheap way of passing the time of day—scenes we know from *A Simple Story* and "Young and Old Together." Contemplating the fate of Mr. Zommer, his innkeeper, he is reminded of how aspiring young spirits became mired in shopkeeper-ish domesticity. Reb Chaim, the one-time Talmudic prod-igy, brings to mind the contentiousness of a self-interested rabbinate and—in the person of Chaim's ex-wife—the mis-ery of young women forced into loveless marriages and matrons' wigs.

As he faces all this, it becomes clear that the Guest is not seeking the town he once knew, as it actually was, but a very different town that has lived in his imagination. This is evident in the very first chapter, in his first response to what he sees: "Every place was changed, even the spaces between the houses. Nothing was *as I had seen it when I was little, nor as it had been shown to me in a dream shortly before my return.*" [4] Everything he observes is in fact measured against thoroughly subjective criteria: "The cantor did not draw out his prayers—or perhaps he did, but that was my first prayer in my home town, and it was Atonement Eve. . . . So I wanted to draw out the prayers even more, and *it seemed to me as if the cantor were cut-ting them shorter all the time.*" [5]

To be sure, what he seeks inwardly is, as I have already noted, not a uniquely personal experience but rather the ge-neric sense of security of the old study-house world. Hav-ing been given the key to the old *beit midrash* (study house), he immures himself there and immerses himself in the old books. For a long time he remains shut up in the study house, savoring a renewed contact with the past and intermittently pondering the relationship to God and his-tory which made the whole loaf of the ancestral civiliza-tion possible. As he struggles to maintain his connection to the old modes, he becomes dimly aware that it is a kind of *transcendent* experience that informs his consciousness. The old order is, after all, a religious order involving an intimate relation to the deity and faith in the utterances that reveal both God's will and Israel's destiny. For the Guest, however, that kind of experience has little to do with concrete moral, historical, or theological imperatives. It has to do chiefly with the "feel" of the experience—a "feel" that is nonetheless bound up with the particular creeds and values.

What the Guest learns about this field of experience is that it lives on within him, and can even be temporarily revived as long as he is immersed in the old texts. But his effort is as problematical as its effects are transient. In accepting the *beit midrash* key, he was realizing a childhood dream about locks and keys, houses and access to houses—about the grown-up world, and his freedom and competence within it.[6] But even as he seeks to satisfy his nostalgia, it becomes clear that the past cannot be recaptured and that in trying to recapture it, he somehow loses touch with his already tenuous present life. To recreate the old sense of wholeness he must abstract himself from the present: from his wife, his children, and from his real involvement with the real Palestine, where he hopes the old values may find a new embodiment.

Yet a considerable part of the Guest's difficulty stems from the fact that the Palestine toward which he intermittently yearns is not the real Palestine, the Palestine he has known. It is, rather, a part of the millenial vision of Eretz Yisrael—the Land of Israel. That vision, as it figures in the Guest's imagination, is no more reality-bound than is his haunting memory of the town. Indeed, his nostalgic image of the old Szibucz is no more idealized than his vision of Eretz Yisrael.

For the Guest constantly plays Palestine against Szibucz, even as he plays the past against the present. Szibucz is cold and its weather is cruel, but Palestine—especially the visionary Palestine—is warm and its climate is benign. One buys moldy potatoes in Buczacz, while in Palestine one eats one's fill of golden oranges. Life in Buczacz is atomized, and its people are cut off from each other. Palestine is a community in which there is a mutuality of interests and concerns. To cleave to the tradition in Szibucz is to live hidebound within the moribund traditions. In Palestine, one is more free to mold the tradition as one wills. Buczacz is the oppressive past, Palestine the glorious future—and so on.

The reality of Palestine, he admits, is very different from his vision of it. We realize that for the Guest there are two Palestines, a "real" one and an "ideal" one. In the real one, the newspapers retail tattle and brother opposes brother; management, as Yerucham Freeman angrily points out, exploits labor, Arab kills Jew, and both Arab and Jewish workers are often on the verge of starvation.

The Guest acknowledges all this. Yet he continues to be haunted by his dream of a golden land with a golden clime, where the millennial vision of redemption can be fulfilled —just as he is haunted by his vision of the *shtetl* culture and experience. Neither dream can be realized within the world that is reflected in this novel. Indeed, both visions may be said to stand in the way of the Guest's immediate satisfactions. Yet both visions and the imaginings they embody continue to have a measure of validity for the Guest

—and for us. It seems difficult to live with such imaginings, but to live without them is inconceivable.

[4]

Indeed, there is a sense in which imagination—its scope, value, and limits—is a dominant theme in the novel. In a conversation with the half-literate Hanoch, the Guest explicitly formulates a conception of that faculty; and his formulation bears on the novel as a whole:

"Do you know what imagination is, Hanoch? . . ." "I don't know," says he. "If so . . . sit down and I will explain it to you. Imagination is something through which everyone in this world lives; you and I and your horse and your cart. How can that be? Well, you go out to the village because you imagine that your income is assured there. The same applies to your horse and the same to your cart, for without the power of imagination the world would not go on living." [7]

In itself, the formulation is primitive enough—but it serves to define the chief actions of the main characters in the novel. Hanoch's imagination is limited, yet it carries him into the snowstorm as he seeks his "income"—that is, his living. And he dies in the snowstorm, as Daniel Bach lost a leg, seeking a "Jewish living." Virtually everyone in the novel, in fact, is moved by the capacity to imagine what will accrue to him by returning to the town or by leaving it. For the Guest is obviously not the only returnee. Indeed, there are so many returnees that the novel may be seen as a complex structure of returns, each motivated in a different way, yet each satisfying a need analogous to all the others. The tailor's wife imagines that her home place will restore her health. Zommer imagines he will somehow be able to take up his former life where he left it. Yerucham Freeman imagines he will be able to institute wholesome changes in its social structure; Aaron Schutzling imagines he will be able to recapture his romantic youth. The narrator imagines he will be able to recapture the experience of "wholeness" he knew in his childhood. And so on.

One of the horrors the narrator confronts is the narrow range of the imaginings that inform the life of his fellow townsmen. His own sensibility, on the other hand, is beset by a bewilderingly broad range of imaginings. When he arrives, he thinks he is merely killing time—is merely between times, as it were. He thinks he is merely visiting the home place. As for Palestine, he seems unaware of how visionary his image of it is. Only with the passage of time does he seem to realize how much he is animated by a richly imagined vision of the past, which he never really escapes. He hopes beyond hope that that vision can be reincarnated in an ideal Eretz Yisrael, rooted in realities he knows to exist.

In a sense, though his imagination carries him away from ordinary reality and even threatens to put him out of touch with it, it also carries him toward a larger, more vital reality. One might say that only the sensibility which, while playing over the present, can fully envision the past, is able to grasp the full tragedy of the present and to move effectively toward the future. Contemplating the people who pass before his eyes in the course of his stay, the Guest glimpses the reality that created them as well as the reality that destroys them.

The people, to be sure, are only dim shadows of the central reality—that is, the reality of the ancestral past. Through them there glimmer, as through a glass darkly, the possibilities of the old, lost, deeply desiderated modes of existence. Old Freide, once his mother's nurse, who becomes an emblem of tender, dauntless motherhood; Hanoch, the plodding hewer of wood and drawer of water, who epitomizes a transcendent faithfulness in direst extremity; Reb Chaim, the lapsed scholar, who embodies the virtues of learning in his fall from learning—these are among the villagers who come to embody the qualities of faith, of fortitude, of gentleness, and of unpresuming dignity which, in the mind of the Guest, characterize the old culture. They, and their virtues, rather than any moral or theological precepts, symbolize the whole loaf of the age-old tradition.

It is not only isolated virtues that these people embody, however. They epitomize the inherited pattern of responses that make up their tradition. Most of them lack the self-consciousness necessary to realize this, as Reb Yudel lacks the self-awareness necessary articulately to grasp the metaphysical symbolism of "The Song of the Alphabet." Those who have the capacity for such self-consciousness are too disoriented to sustain the vision. In the present world of the novel, only the Guest, wayward and fanciful though he is, can achieve a vision of the old civilization.

[5]

It is through the Guest that we glimpse the sensibility that participates in such a civilization. Agnon suggests that such a sensibility, ideally at least, is saturated with elements that unite individual and communal consciousness and put it in touch with ideas and feelings that make for a sense of meaning and continuity in life. These elements may be "real" or "visionary," fanciful or imaginative, but they are somehow felt to constitute the substance of life as it is lived. Ultimately, they point to the past experience of the community, to its transcendent sanction in the present, and to its imperatives for the future. The individual imagination is the unifying medium. It is the medium in which the impulse toward transcendence and communion with the deity arises. Compelled by the ancestral tradition, one makes one's first gropings toward God.

And that tradition no longer exists in its integrity; in the terms of Agnon's old metaphor, "The Song of the Alphabet" is no longer sung. Worse than that, the alphabet itself and all it symbolizes grow increasingly inaccessible. The transmission of the ABC itself has become a problem; even those who can transmit it are in danger of debasing it. The language which has sustained the continuity of faith has passed out of the world with the passing of its material and social underpinnings. All that remains of the tradition are the vision of it, in the consciousness of such men as the Guest; the embodiment of its human virtues, in the persons of people like Yerucham, Rachel, and Shlomo Bach, the pious old man who settles in a kibbutz; and the hope that these virtues can be re-embodied in a visionary Palestine to be created out of the dreams and desires of the most admirable survivors of the folk.

This hope, to be sure, is a highly qualified one. Rachel and Yerucham are not likely to go to Palestine. Shlomo Bach is an old man, and there is no evidence that the young members of his kibbutz will perpetuate his virtues. If we look outside the scope of this novel to Agnon's other Palestinian work, it is clear that the virtues he admires are not of real concern to the Palestine community as he sees it. Hence the vision remains a *vision*—a dream that is validated in the imagination and in the desires, but that lacks firm roots in actuality.

Actuality, for the Guest, is the vast desolation of the present, echoing with ghosts of past realities and past imaginings, and haunted by glimmerings of future possibilities—most of them gruesome. For neither past nor future has palpable embodiment in the present. The Guest's present is chiefly a dimension of consciousness haunted by shades from the past and shifting abstractions of the future. From his point of view, the present is made up of mere simulacra of imagined realities that are rooted in the personal and the communal past—and of evidence of the irrevocable pastness of that past. For the present is filled with beings who negate every value that might survive from the past or who feebly sustain such values in the imminent shadow of death. Increasingly, the Guest's present is filled with a series of nightmares that blur the distinction between the "real" and the "imagined," the past and the present, the sacred and the profane.

The Guest must try to flee the nightmare into which his visit has plunged him. But having fled, and returned to Palestine, he is not free. He continues to be haunted by a consciousness of what he has left behind and by the peculiarity of his relation to it. Moreover, he seems to be haunted by the need to bear witness to what his culture once was and to the horror of what it has become. In a sense, he is one of those men who, alone, survives to tell his tale.

And *A Guest for the Night*, with all its apparent casualness of manner, is the deliberate testament of the past. The

Guests' imagination is a peculiarly apt instrument for such witness-bearing. It is informed by vision as well as by experience; by the imponderable values of the tradition as well as by the palpable sights and smells of childhood; by an idyllic sense of Eretz Yisrael as well as by its realities, as he and Yerucham now acknowledge them. As a result, *A Guest for the Night* comes to be an elaborate elegy on the lost *shtetl* culture. Muted, even gray in its tonalities, it renders the disintegration of the human bearers of that culture, as well as of the culture itself.

But it also conjures the anguish of the Guest, whom we come to see as the ultimate victim of the *shtetl* culture in its decline. Agnon's portrait of the Guest is, in its way, as elaborate as his portrait of the town. Instrumentally, the Guest is a reflector of realities that resist direct representation. Beyond that, however, he epitomizes the dilemmas of an entire generation—the generation whose sensibilities figure in all of Agnon's late, first-person narratives.[8]

[6]
The Guest is a haunted man. He lives outside the pale of the old culture but can belong to no other. He congratulates himself on remaining attuned to the old values, but he has lost contact with the daily patterns of the experience that sustained them. He has in practice rejected the decadent *shtetl* culture but cannot either escape it or become insensible to its fate. Even if he did not seek to re-establish direct contact with its traditions, he could not, except by a heroic act of self-assertion, overlook the doom that has overtaken it. And such self-assertion would make for intolerable guilt.

Agnon spins out the terms of the Guest's dilemma in several areas of his experience. He does this in ways that dramatize the pathos of the Guest's existence, even while they suggest his priggishness and the limits of his sensibility. Hence our sense of the Guest's problematical character as an individual and as a type and—presumably—the ambiguities of Agnon's relation to him.

The Guest is full of contradictions. He craves religious communion but seems incapable of the effort that makes it possible. He observes rituals but is not really pious; he has a plethora of sentiment, but no real commitment to principle or creeds. He celebrates certain virtues but knows that no one can really embody them any more. Rachel and Yerucham Freeman are crucial cases in point. Rachel is the very type of the chaste maiden and virtuous bride, but she is with child when she marries. Yerucham, her husband, is a faithless scoffer, yet—with her—he sets the novel's standard of steadfast love and devotion.

The irony is that Rachel and Yerucham do indeed epitomize these virtues, even though they violate the standards of the old *shtetl* decorum. The Guest would be hypocritical to insist that they do not. At the same time, it would be foolish to pretend that their virtues could have been produced by any other culture. It would be equally foolish to deny that a Yerucham *had* to break with the faith and its pieties. Indeed, *A Guest for the Night* is full of vain pieties, like those of the impoverished ironmonger who pretends to have validated a pedigree going back to Sa'adiah Gaon, who had died childless; or those of the Guest, who wishes to affirm the "princeliness" of Israel in the face of the present impoverishment; or of Leibtsche Bodenhaus, who "improves" the Bible by translating it into neoclassical German couplets.

Yet the Guest, though he acknowledges the hopelessness of real commitment to any of the *shtetl* pieties, cannot abandon his vision of the traditional Way and cannot purge himself of its habits of thinking, feeling, and judging. Hence he continually mouths his priggish pieties as though he affirmed them and in doing so loses credibility with us. "Great is the power of religious duty," he says about a completely conventional reconciliation, "for it makes peace between a man and his neighbor." "I have learned from experience," he says elsewhere, "that there is no accident in the world, since all events are caused by the Almighty." His discourse is peppered with such platitudes, grounded in a faith he obviously does not hold.

Worse still, he is given to fanciful image-making, rooted in the homiletic tradition. The following is typical:

The scrolls of the Law stand silent in the Ark. All love and mercy and compassion are enclosed and enfolded in them. How right it would have been had the door opened suddenly and Hanoch entered alive! Dear brothers, how much good it would have done in Israel in this fallen generation of the poor in faith! Alas, the door did not open and Hanoch did not enter. Heaven forbid that the Gentiles had told the truth when they said the wolves had eaten him.

But even if a sharp sword is laid to a man's throat he should not despair of mercy. The Blessed One can still bring salvation if we know how to arouse mercy.[9]

This is masterful writing, from the strictly literary point of view, capturing as it does a common kind of old-time discourse. But its sentiments call the Guest's integrity into question. The man's homiletic frills and metaphoric trills are so elegant, so full of self-congratulation, that they become unbearable.

And the fact is that the Guest, with his preening fuddy-duddiness and his self-congratulatory thrill of satisfaction whenever he turns a phrase, is himself almost intolerable as a human type. He is full of self-pity and self-indulgence, but he obviously does not like himself and lacks the courage of both his desires and his convictions. He is, moreover, guilt-ridden, though what he is guilty of is never made clear. If one speculates on his psychic constitution, it seems that he is clogged with his own resentments and paralyzed by the animosity that suffuses his being. In this, he is not unlike Hershel Hurwitz and the entire line of Agnon's "modernist" heroes. Presumably, the same psychic elements are at work in all of them. But while Agnon intimates a variety of causes for the Guest's anxiety, there emerges no clear, specific cause.

In part, this is a strength. There is the ring of truth in the lack of any single source for his peculiarities. The Guest is uneasy about his failure to love anything. He seems rightly self-conscious about his niggling self-involvement. His cringing desire to please, combined with his sly malice, suggests the hostility that underlies his seeming detachment. He is, moreover, uneasy about his calling. The Guest is, implicitly, a writer, one who has made epitaphs for the dead but has done nothing constructive for either the living or the dead. In one of his hallucinatory visions, the wraith of a sexton contrasts the Guest's epitaphs with his own activity, which involves, even in death, summoning the faithful to prayer.

Implicitly, the Guest's work is being contrasted with religious and humane works. *A Guest for the Night*, which is itself a kind of epitaph to a dead culture, is being contrasted with lifegiving activity, secular (like Yerucham's) or sacred (like the sexton's). And the Guest seems to feel that he is somehow indulging himself in living out the experience that is rendered in the novel that presumably leads to its creation. He seems to assume that he should be acting to restore the lost culture he contemplates, or should at least be an authentic part of it instead. His sense of alienation from that culture is, moreover, augmented by the most telling source of the guilt to which he is subject: a sense of illicit though vague sexuality, especially as it is elicited by Yerucham's Rachel.

Surely, types like the Guest were produced in the decadence of the *shtetl*. We cannot dismiss him merely because he is unpleasant. Why should Agnon not have rendered what is unpleasant in his witness, as he renders what is unpleasant in the devastated Szibucz? Yet one remains uneasy with the author's elaborate indulgence of his protagonist— with the depiction of a character on such a large scale in the absence of any real effort finally to plumb his psychic or moral depths. The Guest, we come to feel, is an essentially shallow man, full of whimsey and fancy but without the capacity to crystallize his conflicts or to confront them. He is a useful mirror of *shtetl* decay. But he and his feelings bulk too large for us to overlook his failings as a character—or Agnon's failings in rendering him.

For there is something odd, uneasy, and—it seems to me —even dishonest in Agnon's relation to him. The scope he gives the Guest's vagaries, and the sweetness of the discourse attributed to him, suggest an affirmation of sorts. Yet in giving his character's puling pieties free rein, Agnon makes him seem ridiculous. Agnon relates to the Guest much as he had related to Reb Yudel: in a kind of ventrilo-quistic way, impersonating him with such seeming sympa-thy that the ironic effect is somehow undercut. And yet the irony is pervasive and at times corrosive.

Indeed, given the felt sympathy for the Guest, the play of irony often seems largely gratuitous. Agnon's irony is often a defensive strategy; he employs it not only to assault what offends him, but also to protect what is valuable to him. In *A Guest for the Night*, one senses that the fine sen-timental flutings render a cherished set of feelings which distance and detachment can neither touch nor dissolve. Some of the novel's force derives from Agnon's capacity to shape and depict such feelings. But the irony directed against them seems hardly to touch their core. Agnon seems to be embarrassed by the Guest's sentimentality, which is so close to his own, and he wants to show he knows both are problematical. But he has neither the will nor the capacity to probe them.

Agnon's distance does not seem like real distance; his ironic stance seems like a mere posture, struck to avoid con-frontation with the issues at hand. If one can speak of insin-cere irony, Agnon's irony, as it is directed against the Guest, is insincere. It exposes the Guest to ridicule from a point of view so ambiguous that it offers a distorted perspective of him, and little true insight into the pertinent issues. Essentially, it merely clears the way for a sustained elaboration of the Guest's fantasies—which, one feels, are very close to Agnon's own.

And this leaves one uneasy. *A Guest for the Night* is masterly in its juxtaposition of types and its balancing of themes. As with *The Bridal Canopy*, its tight thematic structure imposes strict order on a seemingly random, rambling action and projects a coherent sense of both a world and an experience. It is unique, moreover, in its evocation of the pathos of a civilization in decay and the quiet sympathy of its attention to those who are rent by the decline. Yet the medium of that evocation—that is, the Guest himself and his peculiarly reflective rhetoric—is somehow so unpleasant as to put one off. We come away from this novel wondering whether such a Guest was indeed essential to Agnon's scheme, and whether his obfuscations finally make for such clarity as the novel helps us achieve. And, as with so much else in Agnon, the fascinating fact is that we do not really know.

[6]
Between the Now and the Then:
Yesteryear

A Guest for the Night (1939) intimates the limits of the
Zionist vision; *Yesteryear* (1945) spells them out.[1] Set in
Palestine between 1908 and 1912, it probes the relation between the Zionist dream and the quotidian reality. A study
of regression within the ancestral patterns, *Yesteryear* explores the difficulty of forging a national and individual
identity outside them. Beyond that, it confronts the problem of achieving an ordered vision of an essentially disor-
dered world at a time when faith in the government of
God can no longer be sustained and when no alternative vision has emerged.

[1]
   Yesteryear starts with the experience of one Yitzhak
Kummer, who leaves Szibucz for Palestine in about 1907,
dreaming of self-renewal, self-assertion, and self-fulfill-
ment. Instead, he suffers a total erosion of the will and
comes to betray all the values he professes. Like Agnon's
other weak-willed heroes, he does not seek his fate but lets
it overtake him. He becomes, not a noble farmer-pioneer,
but a casual house painter. Instead of creating, he daubs; instead of transvaluing the old values, he dons the Orthodox
gabardine, marries the daughter of a fanatical butcher, and

dies a dog's death in the heart of rabidly Orthodox Jerusalem.

The action centers almost wholly on Yitzhak and unfolds in the rhythm of his gropings. Yitzhak is an irritating protagonist, and the irony directed against him is corrosive. Descended from Reb Yudel, whose patrimony had been dissipated long before his birth, Yitzhak affirms the Zionist dream. That dream is close to the dream of a golden land with a golden clime which is so focal in the experience of the Guest. "Like the rest of our brothers, sons of the Exile, men of the Second Aliya," the novel opens, "Yitzhak Kummer left his country and his birthplace and his town and went up to the Land of Israel, to build it up from its ruins and to build himself in doing so." [2] Yitzhak, however, is not a builder; he will neither "build the land" nor "be built" in the course of building. Indeed, Yitzhak does not go, but is sent. His impoverished father sends him, not out of sympathy with his ideals, but because he is afraid his other children will be infected by them.

"Yitzhak was a fantast," we are told. "His fancy conjured all that his heart desired." And what did his heart desire? The good life, stereotypically conceived:

The whole Land seemed to him a blessed shrine, and the dwellers therein the Blessed of the Lord. Its settlements nestled in the cover of vineyards and olives, and all its fields were enveloped in grain, its orchards burdened with fruit, while valleys yielded their blossoms, forest trees fluttered under azure skies—and the houses were brimming with song. By day they plow and sow and plant and reap; they gather the grape and gather the olive; they thresh the grain and tread the wine. And toward evening they sit, each beneath his vine and each beside his fig tree, his wife and sons and daughters beside him, joyous in their labour and rejoicing in their habitation, recalling past times, in the Diaspora, even as people do when they remember sorrow in times of joy, to enhance their joy.[3]

The moment Yitzhak sets foot in Palestine, we grasp the idiocy of his dream. He imagines "that all Israel are comrades," even brothers, but he finds Palestine chaotic and full of conflict. The range of human types and communities is bewildering. There are Jews and Gentiles, Moslems and Turks; among the Jews there are Orthodox, agnostic, atheist, socialist, and neutral types. There are converts from Christianity to Judaism and from Judaism to Christianity. There are extraterritorial post offices and territorialist factions. There is class conflict; there are various towns with various mores. And there is a great number of isolated individuals, men who live on the margin of society. Indeed, the novel is honeycombed with solitaries, eccentrics who shun human connections and—in contrast to Yitzhak—struggle alone to forge their destinies.

Agnon is ruthless in undercutting Yitzhak's fantasies. Yitzhak dreams of green pastures but sees barrenness everywhere. He dreams of handsome people harmoniously working their land but sees prematurely aged pioneers wresting a meager living from the soil, or smug landlords exploiting Jewish labor. He feels he is going "home" but is collared by an innkeeper greedy for profit.

There are romantic pioneers, to be sure: people who cut dashing figures and talk about "building the land" and "being built by it." But these, with rare exceptions, are haunters of cafés, purveyors of empty rhetoric, and grumbling malcontents. Sonia, the girl into whose arms Yitzhak

drifts during his sojourn in Jaffa, is typical. She has political
opinions but cannot keep up with current events. Yitzhak
thinks of her as a chaste maiden who has succumbed to his
charms, and he therefore suffers guilt over the affair. She is
in fact drawn to his innocence and drops him the moment
the novelty has worn off.

Yitzhak had indulged in erotic daydreams about his life
in Palestine. He had imagined himself a pioneer hero lifting
the stone from the mouth of a well, so that lovely pioneer
girls would come to love him. He is betrayed in this fantasy as thoroughly as in his others. By the time he has taken
Sonia and violated his dream of chaste virility in the course
of doing so, he has already renounced the pioneer ideal and
become a house painter. He has also drifted into the com-
pany of Jaffa's idlest drifters.

After Sonia, moreover, everything falls apart. Lonely,
guilt-ridden, and depressed, Yitzhak goes to Jerusalem.
There he drifts toward the rabid Orthodoxy of old Jerusalem. Cut off from his Zionist affiliations, he adopts the Orthodox garb, lets his beard grow, and reverts to the traditional practices. Drawn to Shifra, the daughter of one Reb
Feish, a right-wing fanatic obsessed with the evils of Zionism, he sinks into Feish's culture. After marrying Shifra and
enjoying all the pleasures of her milieu, including its rabid
moralism, he is bitten by a mad dog and dies.

Yitzhak's lapse into Orthodoxy and his death are wildly
ironic. A sentimentalist like Hemdat, Yitzhak has no vital
interest in the ancestral faith. After arriving in Palestine, he
drops ritual observance altogether. Though deeply aware
of Reb Yudel and haunted by a sense of his lost heritage,
he thinks of him chiefly in Zionist terms—that is, as a man

who has "gone up" to Palestine—or in terms that invidiously dramatize his failures. Yet he is compulsively drawn to a radical Orthodoxy that not only negates Zionism but is also a grotesque parody of the ancestral Way. Yudel's piety was an affirmation of life and a ground for humane understanding. Reb Feish's fanaticism is hate-filled and life-negating. Feish and Geronam Yekum Purkan, the moralistic ranter in whose ambience Yitzhak dies, are gross travesties of the ancestral Way. They contradict the Yudel ideal much as Jaffa coffee houses contradict the pioneering vision.

Yitzhak's end is pathetic and absurd. He suffers agonies of physical pain and spiritual incomprehension. The narrative voice may be presumed to speak for him: "And now, good friends," it says, "when we examine Yitzhak's life, we stand trembling and full of wonder. This Yitzhak, who was no worse than other people, why was he punished so?" Both the pathos and the absurdity of his suffering are compounded by the fact that he himself, inadvertently, has brought it about. The narrative voice pityingly says, "Yitzhak's end does not spring from his beginnings." [4] Yet we know that it does. His character has not only determined his fate, but his own actions have shaped the instrument of his fate. Yet that determination, for all its rigor, merely heightens the sense of absurdity and inconsequence that the novel conveys.

[2]

For *Yesteryear* is dominated by Balak, the dog who destroys Yitzhak, even as Yitzhak destroys Balak, for it is Yitzhak who unwittingly sets in motion the chain of events that drive Balak mad. Painting a sign one day, he playfully dribbles the words "mad dog" in paint on the back of a neighborhood stray. People, reading the legend, hound the poor brute out of its home territory in Meah Shearim, one of the Orthodox quarters of Jerusalem. Hot, hungry, and homesick, the bewildered creature makes its way back, eager to learn what that little house painter has done to it. By the time it finds him, it has gone stark raving mad; as Balak bites Yitzhak, it imagines that his blood will allay its thirst and bring rain to the parching town.

Balak is a complicated figure—and a many-sided fictive device. His story, running to a hundred and more pages of narrative closely intertwined with Yitzhak's story, is the most striking segment of the novel. Racy, vivid, and elaborated in a variety of styles, it projects an action more colorful and a character (Balak himself) more vivid than Yitzhak. Working in part through the conventions of the beast fable, Agnon comments within the Balak sequence on a variety of social and moral issues and, finally, on the human condition itself. "The face of the generation is the face of a dog," says Rabbi Geronam Yekum Purkan, the fiery preacher from under whose gabardine Balak lunges at Yitzhak, and there is a sense in which this is true. Balak is Yitzhak's alter ego, and his frailties parody the frailties, and incomprehensions both of Yitzhak and of mankind. But primarily he parodies (but also symbolizes) aspects of Yitzhak's experience.

Like Yitzhak, Balak must leave his home place because of a label affixed to him. Like Yitzhak, he drifts, craving the cooking pots and the crackpots of Meah Shearim. Like Yitzhak, moreover, he reflects on his ancestry and, like Yitzhak, he contemplates the mystery of his destiny.

More vitally bound up with the inner logic of Yitzhak's development is the way Balak symbolizes aspects of Yitzhak's psychic life. *Yesteryear* establishes certain rigorous psychological patterns for Yitzhak, patterns that the Balak action dramatically highlights. Yitzhak has lived with his mother's dying kiss on his lips, waiting for a girl to "renew" it. He is passive with women, and frightened of them. When he feels desire for Sonia, he imagines that the dog embroidered on her coverlet is wagging the stick in its mouth. Drawn to Shifra, a chaste *shtetl* type who is cast in the mold of maternal virtue, he hears dogs barking. Indeed, he paints "mad dog" on Balak's back in the dawning of his love for Shifra.

Balak embodies both the aggression and the desire which Yitzhak puts out of his mind. The dog's revelatory function is rather like that of Hershel Hurwitz's crowing cocks. Like Hershel, Yitzhak is gruesomely passive and repressed; quite early, the reader wonders where his assertiveness has gone. Then Balak turns up, externalizing Yitzhak's instincts and symbolizing their vicissitudes in the no man's land outside the limits of Yitzhak's conscious life. Associated with Yitzhak, but also with the fierce moralists of Meah Sherim, Balak is the pariah par excellence. An outcast driven mad *because* of his having been cast out, he symbolizes, not only the fate of the social outcast—perhaps of the Jews themselves—but also the permutations of repressed desire. In the unfolding of the fable, pleasure and rage return in the form of Balak to haunt, torment, and finally to destroy their caster-out. It is, if we wish, the return of the repressed in its most virulent and destructive form.

The psychological portraiture is still more precise. Yitzhak cannot dissociate woman from mother and is therefore subject to the terrors of ingrown virginity and the neural itch. The details of the Balak sequence, when linked to Yitzhak's dreams and the novel's numerous other episodes involving four-legged scavengers, suggest fantasies that arise from this basic confusion. Anger is stirred by desire because of the emasculate and emasculating quality of women and the dread they inspire. Furthermore, it is suggested that for Yitzhak his own desire connotes femininity, so when he desires he also wants to be desired. Balak, associated with repressed, guilt-inducing rage, is, like Reb Feish and Reb Geronam Yekum Purkan, associated with bitches as well. The mad dog of Yitzhak's unconscious is the other side of his bitching desire. When Balak leaps at him from under Geronam's gabardine, Yitzhak is presumably succumbing to his own rage and terror and also to his wish that the violent old puritan take him as a man takes a woman. We feel it is no accident that Balak's assault comes so soon after Yitzhak's marriage.

Altogether, Yitzhak's apparently random drifting, when seen in the perspective of the Balak episode, turns out to be a compulsive pursuit, a quest for something that satisfies a psychic need. Yitzhak's "return to the womb," whose signification is rather obvious in the social and cultural perspectives of *A Simple Story* and *A Guest for the Night*, is motivated by a psychic need as well. A deeply regressive impulse draws him back to Old Jerusalem and its vindictive morality. Marriage to Shifra, psychologically, means dissolution, since it is not erotic fulfillment, but a passive regression beset with myriad terrors, not the least of which are homoerotic.

Indeed, Yitzhak's "end" does cast a rather interesting light on his "beginnings." His imaginative life, we recall, is organized around two poles of masculine identification: Reb Yudel and the ideal Zionist pioneer. Reb Yudel looms out of the remote past, while the pioneer belongs to the distant future. Both serve to highlight his own inadequacy. Yitzhak dreams of pioneer exploits to bolster his flagging manhood. In reality, he has no way of redeeming himself from his impotence. Hence, with the whole force of his personal and communal history driving him, he reverts from the pioneer framework to the Yudel framework. There he finds a viable point of identification—not with the potent but humane Yudel, but with the rabid, impotent Feish. Feish, it seems, can serve Yitzhak's needs in a way that Yudel cannot. Yitzhak does not reject Feish and sinks ever more deeply into his way of life. Presumably, that way can satisfy his need to expiate the guilt he feels for his "unholy" desires. In them, he finds imaginative outlets for pent-up violence—a violence whose repression has unmanned him in the first place, and returns to destroy him in the end.

[3]

Balak is the vehicle for this violence, as he is for all the major elements in Yitzhak's psychic life. Through him, Agnon underscores the fatality governing the apparently random events that issue in Yitzhak's death. Altogether, the dog's presence dramatizes the concatenation of accident and necessity that informs the novel. Furthermore, he is a touchstone for judging the various types, factions, and attitudes that are represented. Finally, as a mad dog, he symbolizes something about the human condition in general.

He is directly identified with the decadent Orthodox of Old Jerusalem, as well as with those who are drawn to them. Pure scavenger, and tainted with all the repulsiveness associated with dogs in the Bible, he is at one with the schismatics whose quarter he inhabits. It is no accident that Feish, posting notices of excommunication against the Zionists, has apoplexy when he hears Balak barking. (Afterward, gray-faced, paralyzed, and dribbling, Feish, suggests the utter impotence of the Orthodox.) Nor is it an accident that Geronam, because of his smell, sound, and emotional "feel," is Balak's favorite, or that Balak cowers under Geronam's gabardine. It is a fine irony that Geronam, with his insistence on divine governance, sees Balak as the scourge of God, sent to punish the Zionists, who redeem the land through human rather than superhuman means.

Balak, though most intimately linked to the reactionary Orthodox, bears on the other segments of the community as well. There is dogginess in Sonia's loves, as there is a yellow dog on her coverlet. And there is dogginess in the gross appetency of the intellectual and erotic idiocies of the times. No one can resist interpreting the Balak phenomenon —that is, the terrifying apparition of a mad dog in Jerusalem in a time of drought—and everyone allegorizes him. Through the Balak story, Agnon satirizes the press on the one hand and the rootless intellectualism of the secular culture on the other; he viciously excoriates the political rhetoric of the secular Zionists, the intellectual pretensions of the cultural revivalists, and the myth-and-ritual speculations of anthropological folklorists.

Most of all, the Balak sequence bears on the problem of meaning and order in history. Urged by the rhetoric of the Orthodox, as well as of the host of others who seek meaning in Balak, we are driven to ask ultimate questions: Who or what makes necessity necessary? Whose ends are served by it? And—most devastating of all—may not such questions about order, cause, and meaning be integral parts of the madness and maddening idiocy of human life itself? Feish and Geronam insist on the government of God and a moral economy in the universe. So do the good, pious people of Jaffa and Jerusalem. The Jaffa optimists believe in a vague sort of progressivist meliorism. Yitzhak's fate undercuts both positions. His sinfulness does not justify his hideous "punishment," and the gratuitous horror of his end undermines faith in the goodness of the world. If we try to think of a shaping power, we must think of it as either aimless and indifferent or as malevolent, working as it does through unsavory agencies, like mad dogs, to attain its end.

The Balak action suggests, if possible, a still more nihilistic possibility. Balak goes mad for many reasons. One decisive factor is his passionate interest in "reason" itself, in the logic of his destiny. As he moves further and further from his normal condition, Balak speculates more and more frantically on fate, free will, divine governance, the logic of creation, and so on. As he deteriorates, he becomes obsessed with the problem of truth itself. He has the notion that the truth can save him. He bites Yitzhak under the illusion that the act of biting him will provide him with both the truth and an outlet for his pent-up rage.

Yitzhak is destroyed—in part at least—because of his unreflecting acceptance of the myths and legends of his culture. Balak, his alter ego, is destroyed—in part at least—by his effort to reflect on the myths and conditions of his life. Balak's reflections are, to be sure, absurd: a parody of bewildered human consciousness, Geronam's as well as Yitz-hak's. Yet, in the end, Balak, whose lucidity exceeds both Geronam's and Yitzhak's, is as badly victimized by myth as anyone involved in Yitzhak's life. The implications are dire. Balak's experience suggests the folly and danger of reflection on the "big questions": on matters of whence, whither, and wherefore—that is, on the human (or, more accurately, the canine) condition. Balak's legends and beliefs are as arbitrary as Geronam's. Either reflection on them or unreflecting acceptance of them makes for idiocy—or madness.

Metaphorically, at least, men are like dogs and dogs are like men: both madden when they try to make sense of their condition, but they also madden when, like Yitzhak, they do not. A man is damned if he struggles to make sense of the world, and damned if he does not. Insofar as Yitzhak *is* Balak, Yitzhak is damned by both acts: by the struggling and the not struggling, by the seeking and the failure to seek.

It is a stark vision that Agnon projects. There is logic in events, but the events themselves are finally incomprehensible. The very effort to comprehend leads to madness. But then, it seems, so does the refusal to try. The power that governs the world may be benign, malevolent, or indifferent. There may be no such power at all. All we really know is that the world is—and we are not even quite firm in our grasp of that knowledge.

[4]

One might expect that the grimness of this vision would be relieved by the fact that it unfolds within the heroic period of Zionist settlement, aspects of which the novel

evokes in some detail. The contrary is true. Agnon acknowledges the success of the Zionist effort in creating a
community and a culture but discredits the possibility of
using it to vindicate any cosmic or historical scheme. Indeed the novel's vision of Zionist history is as nihilistic as its
vision of Yitzhak's doom. The slow, weaving growth of the
Palestine Jewish community is acknowledged, but it is seen
to be as accidental as Yitzhak's fate. Just as Yitzhak's doom
is a matter of indirections and obliquities, of large effects
growing from small causes, so the "happy ending" of the
Zionist enterprise is felt to be a matter of accident, blunder-
ing, inconsequence, or of self-interested manipulation of
random contingencies.

The treatment of the Jaffa community makes this clear.
So does the portrait of Yedidiah Rabinovitch. Yedidiah, Yitzhak's friend and foil, starts out as a convivial pioneer and
ends as a convivial entrepreneur. A principled opponent of
the "exploiting" class, he becomes one of its leading exponents. And he does so by feeding chocolate to a lap dog he
chances on in a German park. This endears him to its mis-
tress, who ends up marrying him. The contrast to Yitzhak is
too blatant to be overlooked: Yedidiah becomes one of the
moving forces of the developing community, and Yitzhak
dies in agony. Yedidiah adapts, and Yitzhak does not. But
Yedidiah's fate, like Yitzhak's, hinges on a dog.

The part played by unintelligent and unintelligible accident is noted still more explicitly in a chapter on the founding of Tel Aviv:

Later, when sightseers came to spy out the land and saw this
bustling new suburb called Tel Aviv, they would never have
imagined that the spot was once utterly desolate . . . , and that

there was so much squabbling among its founders. . . . Tourists think that Tel Aviv has always been what it is now, and each of the founding fathers of the town tends to attribute its splendors to his own efforts. But we who acknowledge the glory of the Eternally Living One, by whose might everything is made . . . and who at will bestows life and mercy and grace —we who acknowledge his power will fill our mouths with laughter at those who, in their ignorance, think that they, with their strength and power and the cunning of their hands, made Tel Aviv what it is. Tel Aviv became what it is by virtue of the life that was in the Eternally Living, in utter contradiction of everything the founders of Tel Aviv would have wished. . . . Otherwise, if they had really wished to make Tel Aviv what it is now, why are its streets so narrow? [5]

The narrative voice undercuts any purposive or providential view of Zionist history. It does so by invoking the fallibility of the founding fathers in simple matters like the width of streets. But it also invokes, recurrently, the "Eternally Living One" and the mysteries of His ways. But the impulse to read history in terms of God's will is, as I have already suggested, in itself problematical. If we pose the question of divine governance, we must consider Yitzhak's death and the logic or justice that underlies it. And if *that* question is asked, belief in the Eternally Living One must be as thoroughly discredited as a meliorist view of history.

[5]

Agnon also undercuts simple acceptance of the narrative voice and its point of view. Even if one admits that there is no apparent design in particular developments, one may nonetheless be tempted to read the concatenation of small causes as the work of Providence. This, for example, is done in *The Bridal Canopy*, where Agnon playfully juxtaposes a comic with a providential view of accident—and asks us, provisionally, to share the providential one. The same method might have been used here, with the difference that Yitzhak's fate involves an ironic-pathetic rather than a comic viewpoint. Thus, the particular moment of the past in which Yitzhak died could be viewed as a moment in a glorious historical process, and his death could be thought of as a sacrifice on the way to greater glories. But Agnon will not let us regard Yitzhak's fate in this way. His irony is too heavy for that, especially at the novel's ending.

For Agnon concludes the novel with a virtuoso parody of such mealy mouthed, addle-pated affirmations as might come naturally to the narrative voice. "With Yitzhak's burial," we are told, "the rains come": first fierce, driving rains, then the "gentle rains—as of blessing." [6] "Only yesterday [*tmol shilshom*, the words that constitute the novel's title] we prayed and we pleaded and chanted the penitential prayers, blowing the rams' horns and reciting the pleas for salvation, and now we recite these hymns of praise with thanks and tuneful song." The rains, we hear, then fell for seven days, and brought the earth to blossom; shepherds and their flocks came to pasture, and farmers plowed their fields:

The Land, it seemed a blessed shrine, and the dwellers therein the chosen of the Lord. . . . Let the mourners mourn this afflicted soul, . . . but we will recount the deeds of our sisters

and brothers, children of a living God, who work the soil of
Israel's land for pride and praise and glory.
Yitzhak's deeds are done.

> Those of our other comrades will
> follow in the book *A Portion of the Field*.[7]

There is, so far as we know, no work entitled *A Portion
of the Field*. The sequels that Agnon sometimes announces
at the end of his novels and tales—like the account of Blumah Nacht's life that is promised at the end of *A Simple
Story*—never appear. One senses that a sequel never *could*
appear, given the self-contained conclusiveness of the
works in question. The promise of more to come seems to
be an element of the pervasive ironic technique—in this
case, the technique of playing into our puling-pious wishful
thinking. Such thinking (and feeling) is parodied in the
simpering simplism of "Let the mourners mourn . . . ; *we*
will tell of the doings of our brethren." [8] This is rendered
absurd by the whole of the novel. It involves a reversion to
the rhetoric with which *Yesteryear* begins, a rhetoric
which the entire novel, with its weirdly compassionate but
ironic account of Yitzhak's "deeds," makes impossible.

For, as in *A Simple Story*, Agnon here adopts the commonplace, pietistic rhetoric of the milieu he is rendering
and parodies it to the point of utter incredibility. The novel's story is told from the viewpoint of a mildly pious,
mildly Zionist type who assumes the existence of a *we* that
automatically enters into its sentiments. It opens by referring to "our brothers, the sons of the Exile, men of the Second Aliya," and reverts to the first-person plural viewpoint

from time to time throughout. But having seen the nature of the *we*, and the nightmarishness of the immediate world in which the *we* subsists, the reader cannot accept so moral and meaningful an account of the relation between Yitzhak's fate and the history of the Zionist community. By no stretch of the imagination can Yitzhak be thought of as a sacrificial victim whose death brings rain and the fertility that rain assures.

[6]

And yet, by one of those further twists of irony of which he is a consummate master, Agnon makes us feel that the narrative voice, though silly and unreliable in its reading of events, at least respects the incomprehensible mysteries. It does have a sustained sense of life and death as awesome, inviolable realities. It assumes, with the benign Orthodox people of the novel—Reb Alter, Shifra, Shifra's mother Rivka—that death, like life, must be accepted as part of the given scheme of things, and that any strenuous effort to understand it will result in failure, if not madness. And this concept of experience—especially against the background of all the idiotic logic-chopping and sentimental evasion that the novel renders—is the only viable one.

For the novel, with all its ironies, looks lovingly and longingly to the ancestral attitudes, which made it possible for men to transcend their petty egotism and accept the mysteries of life and death. Those who, in the present of the novel, naïvely invoke the rhetoric of Providence and divine governance are, to be sure, absurd or pathetic. But there hovers in the background of the novel a sense of another mode of response—the Yudel mode, in all its ramifications. Yitzhak has lost touch with it; Feish and Geronam can only travesty it. The latter merely daub over a dead tradition, as Yitzhak daubs the crumbling walls of Jaffa and Jerusalem. Yet that tradition survives, woefully inadequate but *there*, providing a perspective in which to place everything that informs the life of this novel. That perspective reminds us that there is an ultimate standard against which events, values, and people can be judged.

That standard may be regarded as an obscurantist one. It implicitly affirms the vision enunciated by the voice from the whirlwind when it undercuts Job's rationalist effort to darken wisdom without understanding. Like the voice from the whirlwind in the Book of Job, the benign Orthodox characters in this novel affirm that some sort of order governs the universe, but that the rules of that order are not finally comprehensible. At the same time, they feel that accountability is possible, so that Reb Alter, an elderly circumciser from Szibucz, contemplating Yitzhak's death, can question its justice and reflect on its pathos. But the implicit sense of order and pathos is such that neither Reb Alter nor any of his compeers has the illusion that he can penetrate the mystery of the divine will and its ways. Adhered to without sentimentality, such a view offers no easy solace but makes it possible to submit, complain—and carry on.

Belief in such a view is shared by the handful of gentle pietists ranged around Shifra and her mother: kindly folk who are lost among the aggressive moralists of old Jerusalem and even persecuted for their kindliness, but who insist on pursuing their vision and their way. For them the world is radically coherent, very like Reb Yudel's world. Indeed, Reb Alter invokes the concept that underlies "The Song of the Alphabet." Speaking of the rhymes he made at Yitz-hak's parents' wedding, he notes the way that the coupling of sounds in rhyming verse is the prototype of the coupling of man and woman in marriage, a coupling that prefigures the larger harmonies of the world.

Yet the fact is that, even though Reb Alter affirms the old vision, the vision itself has lost the power of self-per-petuation. Indeed, as *Yesteryear* portrays the exponents of the old, benign Orthodoxy, it conveys an anguished sense of the mutability of the tradition. It confronts Yudel's tra-dition, moreover, not with the riddles of poverty and wealth or order and disorder, as in *The Bridal Canopy*, but with the mystery of life and death: with a tragic world, that is, in which tragic actions are no longer possible.

In evoking the possibility of order and meaning, *Yester-year* projects an insight that had already been enunciated in *The Bridal Canopy:* that is, an awareness of the extent to which the ancestral mode is a made mode, though not a willed one. *The Bridal Canopy* showed how the ancestral tradition was a conventional one, but conveyed a sense that the conventions were unwilled. They were given, and men worked unselfconsciously within them. Though arbitrary, such conventions were able to impose a coherent system of meanings on life. Yudel and his peers could argue about the meaning of particular circumstances, but the overall frame-work of meanings was clear.

In *Yesteryear*, as in all of Agnon's modern fiction, Yu-del's assumptions no longer hold, even for most of those who practice the faith. They no longer define the whole of life. The structure of vision has been warped, so every man can fabricate any meaning he cares to as he confronts "reality." Such meanings do not "hold," however, because the central core and outer frame of meaning do not hold.

For Yudel, as for the journalistic and pietistic allegorists of *Yesteryear*, everything that passes is only a parable. But Yudel's parable has fixed terms of reference. In *Yesteryear*, where there are no fixed terms of reference, anything can mean literally anything. This is made clear in the elaborate systems of meaning attached to the Balak phenomenon as journalists, politicians, theologians, ethnologists, anthropologists, poets, and just plain folks latch onto the fact that a mad dog is loose in drought-afflicted Jerusalem. Readers have interpreted the satire on allegories that is worked into the Balak sequence to mean that nothing has any meaning —that it is foolish to probe the meaning of the Balak episode, as of anything else. Thematically, this interpretation has a measure of validity, to the extent that it accords with the novel's nihilistic sense that it is futile and even mad to probe meanings.

Yet the Balak episode in itself *has* meaning—and a fairly clear, though not wholly definable, meaning. And one of its meanings is that meaning itself is problematical in Jaffa, Jerusalem, and Szibucz of circa 1910—in effect, the modern world. Indeed, the novel itself "imitates" in its style and structure the problem of interpreting the significance of events. Much of the novel is clouded with meanings, but these meanings have no fixed point of reference in the world that is depicted. All one knows with certainty is that life is replete with compulsions and ironies, and that men can at best struggle to wrest some semblance of meaning and value in the shadow of death, desperation, and absurdity.

The only person in the novel who perhaps begins to confront the full complexity of life and its absurdities—including the absurdity of death itself—is a painter called Blaukopf. He is one of the many young men who serve as foils to Yitzhak. Blaukopf, a Galician who helps Yitzhak in Jerusalem by teaching him the art of sign painting, dies of tuberculosis at thirty. His death, painful and prolonged, is in clear contrast with Yitzhak's. Because of Blaukopf's fondness for the tradition, his background, and his early death, the drama of the contrast is considerable. While Yitzhak drifts unconsciously, full of vague fears and longings, the amiable Blaukopf has strong will and a rich consciousness of the radical issues of his life. Furthermore, he has the need to wrest some meaning from his life and to convey it to others. Aware that he is dying, he works to the very end, painting an allegory of life: a visionary painting, in which a snake and a tiger are coiled in mortal combat. The tiger is death and the snake is life; life, in this case, is trying to choke the life out of death. Blaukopf's sympathies, presumably, are with the tiger, death.

The concomitant of Blaukopf's vital relation to death is a vital relation to life. He is the novel's only happily married man in Yitzhak's generation, and he is one of the few people who not only can extend affection, but also sustain it. Despite the ironies of his fate, he seems to serve as a touchstone to indicate the possibilities of life and consciousness: a touchstone that reveals the unpredictability, the disarray, the waste, and the pain that inform life itself, but also the dignity that honest exertion of one's God-given faculties can bring. His death is as absurd and unearned as Yitzhak's. But he is able to meet it with a sense of its incomprehensible dignity, and hence of his own dignity as a man—a mortal.

Blaukopf is the only modern man in the novel who achieves anything like a viable relation to the realities of life, death, and history. He differs from the benign Orthodox in that he faces the horrors of existence without the consolation of faith. Blaukopf has looked into the abyss and tried to salvage something from it. It is not his fault that the paintings in which he has recorded his vision are left to rot after his death. He has at least striven and has possibly, for a moment, triumphed in the spirit. To do more than that, in the world that Agnon depicts here, seems inconceivable.

For the novel is pervaded by a sense of life as the quintessence of dust—of offal, perhaps—a life which can be redeemed only by the struggling human spirit, and then only if it is not preoccupied with survival or self-perpetuation by inappropriate means. *Yesteryear* pillories the obsession with self-perpetuation and the constricting egotism it springs from in a great variety of ways. At one point, for example, we hear of a hyena who allows himself to be killed and stuffed because he thinks taxidermy confers immortality. The taxidermist who is said to have stuffed him —one Arzef, whose name literally means "hellebore"—has the illusion that he really preserves his beasts and presumably believes that he advances knowledge by classifying them, even as Rechnitz, in "Betrothed," believes he serves knowledge by drying out the rich "fruits of the orchard of the sea" and classifying them scientifically. Yitzhak himself drips the words "mad dog" on Balak's back while painting a sign that is meant to "immortalize" a philanthropist who has founded an orphan asylum.

Indeed, there is the sense in the novel that every effort to fix meanings or values or to arrest the transience of life is touched with madness. Arzef makes the attempt, as do the ethnologists and anthropologists on whom Agnon casts a satiric eye. So, grotesquely, do the people who take the lovely seashell picture frames that Blaukopf once made and fill them, not with visions, but with portraits of politicians, writers—and themselves.

These are all people who shore themselves up against oblivion, attempting to intermit the flow of time and life and to assure the survival of something of their own in the face of death. It is at the petty egotism of such as these that Agnon directs his hyena snarl. Yet the alternative to petty self-seeking and niggling self-involvement is not pursuit of glory or conscious altruism. It is the humble way of Yitzhak's forebears, who had the faith and the courage to abandon themselves to the drift of God's mercy. Since that Way is closed, there is nothing but suffering and solitude —and, for the chosen few, the struggle to wrest some meaning from both. Such a struggle depends on the recognition of one's nullity.

Agnon is relentless in his ironic insistence, in his covert, ironic insistence on the need for such humility. *Yesteryear* evokes, to be sure, the evanescent sweetness of the ancestral Way. Some of its characters, like its narrative voice, are full of nostalgia for it and for the easy conviviality of the pioneer days. But Agnon gives them no quarter. There *is* no way back, and no communal substitute is available. Some individuals may hear strains of a siren song that carries them beyond their fatal modern circumstance. But those strains, the novel suggests, lead nowhere. Agnon's late novellas may suggest realities in the soul and in the cosmos that lure one beyond the everyday and the commonplace. *Yesteryear*, however, admits of no such possibility. Everything in it lives under the sign of death, decay, and bestiality, even—perhaps especially—the Zionist dream.

[7]
"The Whole Loaf":
Tales of the Modern World

Agnon's world is full of solitaries. It abounds in beggars
and gravediggers, poets and peddlers, in husbands provisionally separated from their wives, and wives eternally cut
off from their husbands. Even Reb Yudel, though he is
deeply cocooned in the ancestral vision, engages Agnon's
fancy partly because of the figure he cuts as a wanderer on
the roads of Galicia.

Reb Yudel and the other people of the traditionalist tales
are, to be sure, very different from the solitaries of the
modernist work. Menashe Haim, in "The Crooked Made
Straight," encounters a series of deathly figures at a fair,
and we know that they signify his mortality—and our own.
He wanders from place to place, a stark and lonely figure in
an unsympathetic universe, and we apprehend the essential
solitude of our condition. Yet, even in his isolation, Menashe Haim sustains a vital relation to the deity and his
Way. He has wandered out of the conventional, middle-
class world; he has even, in his gluttony and then in his failure to claim his wife as his own, strayed from the path of
strict virtue. Yet he continues to be cradled in a comprehensive system of values, values that assure him of the reality of contact with something beyond himself, something
that sustains the universe itself.

The solitaries of the modern world know a more radical isolation. They are cut off from their fellows, but also from any firm relation to anything substantial beyond themselves. Their psychic and spiritual isolation is often dramatized by their urban environment, which makes for much jostling but little contact. And their basic vulnerability is signified in the dreams to which they are subject: dreams whose content they cannot interpret or share, and which capture the essential loneliness of their condition. They do not confront death and mutilation as much as loneliness, bad dreams, and debilitating anxiety.

[1]

Yesteryear, which offers the most richly elaborated account of what we recognize as the modern world, is dominated by such solitary types. Leichtfuss (Lightfoot) lives by the sea with his dog. He works at whim and only suffers women to visit him occasionally. Arzef (Hellebore), a misanthrope, lives alone in the hills outside Jerusalem, stuffing dead animals and shunning men because of their equivocal morality. Menachem (Consoler), an idealized scholar-pioneer, communes only with his Talmud and his farm implements. Hemdat (Desired One, or Desirer) lives in a room with the sea on one side and Jaffa on the other and strives to be a poet. And Balak, mad and thirsty, casts his grotesque shadow over them all.

Set apart from society, the solitaries of *Yesteryear* nonetheless epitomize the real nature of society. The world of *Yesteryear* is essentially incoherent and provides no stable frame of social or spiritual reference for those who drift within it. Its deepest problems are explored through Yitzhak-Balak, but Hemdat, the lonely romantic poet, exemplifies them in a more universalized way. Like Yitzhak, Hemdat is tossed hither and yon, uncertain about his nature and his place; like Yitzhak, he is sociable but full of incommunicable fantasies; like Yitzhak, he would like to join the crowd but is restrained by shyness and his involvement with his feelings.

Hemdat, though a minor character in *Yesteryear* and one of the least interesting, is central to Agnon's conception of modern man and the conditions of his existence. He appears in several tales as the bewildered poet who no longer lives within the ancestral culture and must therefore evolve an autonomous sense of his culture and himself.[1] As a man of imagination, he must conjure "the thing that is not"; he must, moreover, distinguish between substantial and insubstantial fictions. He therefore has to engage in a kind of incessant activity in which the objects of his striving are not evident. For this reason he lives in a shadowy world of incipient, imminent achievement. He could, presumably, lapse into absurdity like Leibtsche Bodenhaus in *A Guest for the Night*, who is dedicated to versifying the Scriptures in German couplets, or like Notkiss in "Young and Old Together," who translates the local burial society's regulations into medieval German. At the same time, it is conceivable that, like Ginat of "Ido and Enam," he might find himself transcribing the primordial music of the human soul. But how is he to know?

Like other twentieth-century writers, Agnon takes the artist's situation as typical of the modern, isolated individual's. He never explores his artists in depth, however, as he at least begins to explore Hershel and Yitzhak. Rather, he takes his situation and notes its problems: problems that are examined more fully in his treatment of other characters.

It is the problems of Hemdat's situation, however, that concern me here. As an artist, Hemdat must create his own "myths," his own images, and his own patterns of discourse. Unlike "our fathers," he cannot work within all-encompassing, universal schemes. Nor can he be satisfied with adding insights and emendations to the substantial body of extant lore. He must confront a range of characteristically modern problems. Can one transcribe reality by recording it as it is? Can language itself be relied upon to convey it—especially the fumbling, newly revived Hebrew he wishes to use? But where does reality lie in the first place? If it lies in oneself, how does one externalize it? What does one's inwardness have to do with other people's? What reality can one attribute to the images that surge out of the inner recesses of one's being?

Hemdat's plight is compounded by the fact that his world is utterly incoherent. The Palestine community consists of unreflecting, self-interested, or passive people, whose standards and values command no respect, and who lack a vital relation to each other or to their culture. Yitzhak's fate suggests that unreflecting adherence to the old structure of values dooms one to chaos. As in *A Simple Story*, only withdrawal seems honorable. The free individual—the thinker, the artist, the scholar—must define himself in solitude. But solitude guarantees nothing, since it swarms with all the problems that Hemdat, Yitzhak, and the Guest must face.

For what is true of the outright *isolados* of Agnon's fiction is true—though to a lesser degree—of its ordinary men. Agnon's twentieth-century people live in a present which has lost touch with the meaningful past and its communal imperatives. To the extent that they have not retreated into utterly private worlds, they—like the Guest—are torn between a past they cannot recapture and a present to which they cannot relate. Cut off from the ancestral satisfactions, they are hounded by guilt about the ancestral culture, but also about neglecting the present because of their fixation on the past. In the present, they are often unable to make satisfactory contact with others. Like the Guest, they often find themselves separated from their families. In general, they cannot depend on others to share their responses. Indeed, such otherness as presents itself to their consciousness often seems so alien and grotesque that the outside world comes to seem spastic and demented. Cut off from invigorating contact with it, they remain at the mercy of their inner, often regressive compulsions.

Their solitude is thus an inner phenomenon, but not a willed one. Apart from those who, like the scholars of the late parables, in a sense choose their isolation, most of Agnon's people suffer an unwilled solitude. They live in an anxiety-ridden, dreamlike state in which they cannot distinguish the real from the imaginary, and in which radical regression is a constant threat. The more they struggle against their regressive impulses, the more such impulses come to dominate them, so that the will is paralyzed and activity comes to seem futile or meaningless. Indeed, the more deliberate the struggle for control, the more complete the devastation. The horror is compounded by the sense of the radical, even the apocalyptic, corruption and bestiality of the world. It is a world to which they cannot belong, but from which they cannot be wholly alienated.

Agnon's modernist tales deal with the themes that inform all his twentieth-century fiction. They are concerned with the loss of substantive ethnic identity, with the loosing of the bonds of community, with the difficulties of orienting oneself to an alien and potentially hostile world. Again and again they touch on the terrors that attend upon the loss of transcendent sanctions for existence, and the horrors of a Godless world. Details of action and character generally reflect the specifically Jewish quandary, but even when they do not very strikingly do this, the immediate ambience of language and image draws us back into the Judaic frame of reference. The Jewish dilemma serves, however, as a base for a more comprehensive vision of modernity. That vision involves the rootlessness, the passivity, and the unredeemed isolation of a world that has come to embody objectively the worst dreams of solitude and disjunction. That disjunction involves a severance from the center of human connectedness that Agnon envisions in the context of the ancestral faith.

[2]

"The Book of Deeds," written between 1932 and 1945, epitomizes the nightmarish sense of the "no world," in which modern man, as Agnon sees him, subsists.[2] Made up of twenty tales, the most elaborate less than twenty pages long, it renders dreamlike states of bewilderment and disorientation, not unlike those in Kafka's work. The stories center upon a nameless first-person speaker who, like the Guest, shares some of the qualities the reader immediately recognizes as Agnon's own: a tropism toward the past; a present existence in a shadow world where Buczacz and Jerusalem tend to mix and mingle; a petty, guilt-inducing egotism; a susceptibility to feelings of guilt; and a comically chronic incapacity for effective action. These qualities and their subjective reverberations are the central human concern of the "Book."

The title "The Book of Deeds," like so many of Agnon's other titles, is scathingly ironic. "Deeds" suggests positive religious as well as profane action, and any kind of action seems virtually impossible here—most of all, acts of real piety, in any sense. The tales vary widely in detail, but they characteristically involve missions accomplished late, badly, or not at all. Many of the stories involve lapses in ritual observance—especially that connected with the Day of Atonement and the ritual cleansing of guilt. Altogether, there is mounting terror at the failure to act, and to act expeditiously. In the earliest of the tales, for example, the narrator sets out to get a doctor for his sick father and sister, but lets himself be waylaid by a man called Andermann, whose name ambiguously suggests one of the devil's own names. In another, he thinks he wants to go home to his wife but finds he has forgotten his own address. In a third, he misses the last bus home because he is busy talking with his grandfather. In several he wants to bathe on Sabbath eve, or to get to synagogue on New Year's Day, Atonement, or the Sabbath.

Even where an action is completed, however, tension and anxiety prevail. The center of interest lies, not so much in the act itself, as in the absence of stable points of spatial, temporal, and emotional reference for both the actor and his actions. The outer world of these tales is as fluid as the protagonist's inner world, and as full of incipient threats. "The Book of Deeds" is set in a series of shifting dreamscapes in which the unlikely and the uncanny have the immediate plausibility of ordinary events, while ordinary events have an air of hallucinatory strangeness. Thus the overall tone is one of muted apprehension, mounting to peaks of occasional terror, related to nightmarishly intermittent desire. The recurrent deflection from aims and objects results in anxiety. This anxiety is enhanced in the speaker and the reader by uncertainty about the meaning of people, places, and events, and compounded by the reader's intuitive certainty that they are nonetheless a real part of the speaker's experience. We sense that the events of the tales are projections of his psychic life.

Indeed, the action of the tales consists of externalizations of seemingly unresolvable conflicts. "The Whole Loaf," which is probably the best known of the tales in this mode, epitomizes both the mode, with its ambiguously suggestive dreamlike symbolism on the one hand and its quasi-allegorical thrust on the other, and the problems of interpreting it.[3]

The protagonist of "The Whole Loaf" is alone. His family is away, and he has not prepared food for the Sabbath, so he has not eaten all day. On Saturday afternoon he goes out to eat. On the way to the restaurant he sees one Dr. Yekutiel Ne'eman (Faithful), who asks him to post some letters. The protagonist says he will, but he cannot decide what to do first—eat or mail the letters. As he temporizes, one Mr. Gressler comes along, riding in a carriage and running down pedestrians. To avoid meeting Mr. Hofni, a man who talks incessantly about his mechanical mousetrap, the protagonist grabs the reins of Gressler's team, and overturns the carriage. For a while the protagonist and Gressler grapple in the dust, but the former, fearing for Ne'eman's letters, gets up. Anxious not to miss his meal, he proceeds to a restaurant and orders "a whole loaf." The meal never comes. The speaker spends the night in the empty restaurant, watching rats and cats gnaw the bones that are heaped in front of him and wondering whether they will have a go at him as well. In the morning, he finds himself in the street, hungrier than ever, with the letters—sullied but unopened—still in his pocket.

One of Agnon's more skilled readers, Baruch Kurzweil, has offered a schematic allegorical reading of the tale.[4] Ne'eman is a Moses figure, whose book may be said either to have been dictated by "Lord (. . . .)"—i.e., the Tetragrammaton—or to have been fabricated out of whole cloth. The letters are the Mosaic commandments. Gressler, a worldly man is a diabolic, a Mephistophelean figure. The protagonist, whose distance from the tradition is symbolized by his failure to prepare for the Sabbath, is caught between God and the devil. His hunger is mere appetite, and diabolical appetite at that. Hence it cannot be satisfied and threatens to consume him morally. The gnawing of the rats is remorse —the gnawing of conscience caused by, among other thing, the sexual impulses of the man whose wife is absent.

Another reading, by Arnold Band, insists that the whole loaf refers to the Sabbath loaf and by analogy to the pleasures of the world to come.[5] Hence the narrator's desire for the whole loaf must be seen as nostalgia for the ancestral Way and as a yearning for heavenly bliss. Frustration follows from failure to prepare for the Sabbath, a day which prefigures the world to come. That is, the protagonist's frustration stems from failure to observe the commandments which are the way to life. According to this view, the speaker fails because he seeks the ends without employing the appropriate means.

Both readings elucidate elements of the tale but overlook its crucial ambiguities. Dr. Ne'eman is stuffy, officious, and of equivocal authority: he may "be" Moses, but part of the protagonist's problem lies in the possibility that Moses himself may be a fraud. Both Ne'eman and Gressler, who is apparently Ne'eman's antagonist, belong to the series of officious authority figures to which the protagonist is drawn. The latter, to be sure, accepts the charge of mailing Ne'eman's letters and feels that matters of great urgency, even of life and death, may be involved. But he is not certain about this either.

The power of the tale stems from the fact that the protagonist seems to be in conflict both about mailing the letters and eating his meal; both activities generate intense anxiety. This anxiety is augmented by a somewhat childlike dependency on both Ne'eman and Gressler, as it is complicated by (and expressed through) what one takes to be a quasi-erotic involvement with—and dependent resentment of—them both. As in other tales, the protagonist feels a helpless attraction to rather worldly, authoritative men—like Andermann (Other Man) in "To the Doctor," or Gedaliah Klein (Great God Little) in "The Letter." Whether they are associated with rigor and the Law, like Ne'eman, or with laxity and self-indulgent defiance of the Law, like Gressler, such men are in most of the tales contrasted with the protagonist's gentle, beloved grandfather. The latter, in turn, is associated with the whole loaf—that is, with the ecstatic, melting sweetness of the old ways, the old prayers, the old contacts—indeed, with all the pleasures of the lost ancestral order. The grandfather does not figure in "The Whole Loaf," but the craving for the whole loaf itself seems to replace him.

And indeed, the nightmarish climax of the story, with the dark restaurant, the gnawed bones, the mice, and the felt threat of extinction, suggests a witches' Sabbath of instinctual guilt. Such guilt, presumably, springs from the erotic and the aggressive impulses underlying the radical conflict of the tale—a conflict connected with the speaker's wish to satisfy his most primitive ingestive needs in the wrong place, at the wrong time, and in relation to the wrong people.

Such a conflict informs a wide variety of these tales, whether they are directly concerned with ritual observance or atonement, or with more mundane pursuits. Whatever their particular action, the tales of "The Book of Deeds" are pervaded by a sense of the precariousness of existence; of exile from grace, security, and satisfaction; and of the perpetual but oblique threat of imminent extinction. This is as much the case in the tales which end "happily"—that is, in which the speaker achieves a state of ecstatic union with some aspect of the ancestral world, a union that is closely akin to the transcendent communions of the traditionalist tales. Yet here, in the modernist tales, even while the conveyed sense of satisfaction is great, we are uneasy in relation to it. What, we wonder, is being communed with? Why does the communion make for utter abstraction from present circumstance? Is there any connection between the totality of the communion and difficulties experienced by the protagonist when he is impelled toward the past?

If one contemplates such questions, it strikes one that Agnon is drawing upon a residue of very primitive fantasy that satisfies a set of deeply regressive impulses. Recurrently, the tales reflect the wish to tear down a gross and worldly father figure and to commune with a gentle, unworldly grandfather presence. Such wishes, surfacing at inconvenient times, disrupt adult life and create a sense of helplessness and impotence in their victim so long as he is under their control. Some of Agnon's readers would have it that he is concerned primarily with rendering a condition involving the "death of God" and all that follows from it. Rather, it seems to me, he is evoking the underlying psychic responses that inform the condition of lostness that a moribund tradition and an inaccessible deity imply. In effect, he cuts under the formal, existential quandary to its emotional roots in his culture. The problem of such loss figures in his work, but the major emphases seem to me to be psychological rather than metaphysical.

For Agnon is directly concerned with a psychological condition that reflects the more comprehensive spiritual one. The protagonist of "The Book of Deeds," though there is no explicit biography of him, is subject to the strains that Agnon explores with greater particularity in *A Guest for the Night* and *Yesteryear;* indeed, the stories themselves at times seem like preliminary exercises for these novels. What is striking about the protagonist here bears on the experience of Yitzhak Kummer and the Guest: the way his psychological constitution reflects his historical and spiritual circumstances. The protagonist of "The Book of Deeds" is, like Yitzhak and the Guest, a victim of modern Jewish history. He is cut off from the world of his origins, which has decayed or disappeared, but he is unable to shed his longing for that world. Yet it is clear that his bond to that world is such that, even if that world still existed, he could not tolerate renewed contact with its realities. For his entire being is pervaded by guilt-provoking conflict, which cuts him off from whole-hearted participation in anything —past, present, or future.

Hence, too, the sense of childlike dependence at the center of "The Book of Deeds." The protagonist of its stories is rendered impotent by the force of his unresolved, childlike desires. Yet he is pitiable partly because his terrors are not wholly fantastic. It may be his own pattern of conflict and desire that makes him seek his father's house or the old study house. But *we* know that the object of his quest no longer exists in fact, though it may live on in fantasy. Hence, in the world of fact, even the most manly of men would not be able to restore it. We see, in "To the Doctor," how the protagonist's own distractibility prevents him from getting a doctor for his sick father, but we also sense that his father's ailment may well be symbolic of something still more dire. This "something" has to do with the nightmares of twentieth-century Jewish life, as they are reflected in the tales of the collection; with the horrors, not only of the lost past, but also of the living present of the thirties and forties: midnight arrests; strangulating red tape and bureaucracy; refugees displaced, without passports or hope; Auschwitz' survivors and guilts; poignant nostalgias and numbing griefs; and the loss of a tradition and its deity.

This bond to history is the source of the peculiar pathos of "The Book of Deeds." We move imaginatively within its dreamscape, but we know the relation between that dreamscape and the historical world. More horrible than the secret-service officer's grilling of the speaker in the tale is the world of the Gestapo and the NKVD outside; more gruesome than the office where the speaker is stranded for three days seeking papers for a refugee are the actual consulates of the thirties. Though the larger public realities are rarely explicit, "The Book of Deeds" invokes them obliquely. And as in the experience of the Guest, the very fact that we cannot put them out of mind makes the nuances of the speaker's personal subjectivity and his personal *Angst* seem both more poignant and more absurd. They are seen against the larger backdrop, the apocalyptic one. Because we know the historical palpability of the apocalypse, the protagonist's fragility seems more human, more valuable, and more significant. It reflects the inwardness of one who cannot confront the final horrors of history because, like the Guest in *A Guest for The Night,* he is too frail, too petty, too self-involved—a man whose guilt, like the Guest's, seems rooted in an ineffectual, emasculating egotism.

|3|
We speak of the "world" of "The Book of Deeds," but strictly speaking "The Book" has no coherent world—that is, no consistent dimensionality of time and space. Rather, it presents a dreamscape reflecting a particular consciousness and externalizing a particular subjectivity. Yet to speak of it in wholly subjective terms is to overlook the sense of a historical *world* that it conveys. "The Book of Deeds" plunks its protagonist into the midst of more or less recognizable scenes, generally either in old Buczacz or new Jeru-

salem. It is a world that provides few signposts for positive self-orientation but that is palpably *there* in its immediate particulars, as particular scenes and settings are palpably *there* in our dreams. What is most striking about the setting of "The Book of Deeds" is the generalized sense of ugliness and incoherence and the threat-laden sense of disembodiment within the contemporary scene. The collection projects an experience of disorientation in an "anywhere" which is felt to be the "modern" world.

The "anywhere" modernity of "The Book of Deeds" receives a local habitation and a name in "Thus Far" (1951 and 1952), one of Agnon's last published novellas.[6] The place is the Berlin of World War I, where the first-person narrator is stranded and where he must confront a wholly alien, wholly corrupt universe. "Thus Far" is a panoramic account of a Berlin disrupted by war, as seen by a man who feels no affinity for the city but who has lived in it for a long time and has—though marginally—participated in some of its obscenities. "Thus Far" lacks the inner coherence of Agnon's best work. It is especially interesting, however, because of the way it suggests the grounds of the narrator's affinity for this milieu, even while it enunciates his complete alienation from it and his isolation within it.

"Thus Far" elaborates the motif of homelessness on a heroic scale. Its first-person protagonist, who has been writing a compendious history of man's clothing through the ages, cannot find decent lodgings. He settles into a pension run by a widow, only to be evicted when her shell-shocked golem of a son, turns up—ironically enough, through the narrator's unwitting means.

A frantic quest for satisfactory lodgings then begins—a

quest that does not succeed until the protagonist reaches Jerusalem, and even then, "not by my own merits . . . but for the sake of . . . [the] books." [7] The failures have an almost paranoid quality. Wherever the protagonist settles, he finds that his dwelling has a grotesque flaw. In one, an amputee clumps overhead on his peg leg. Another is so befouled by the smells of thirty-six cookshops and the clatter of the trolley terminal opposite that he cannot open his windows and therefore cannot tell the time of day or the season. The landlady of a third breeds dogs, so dog hairs get into his coffee, his soup, and whatever he touches.

The treatment of the lodging theme involves a grotesque animation of a motif that figures everywhere in Agnon—from the homelessness of Menashe Haim in *The Crooked Made Straight*," to that of the protagonist of "The Whole Loaf." The symbolic ramifications of the motif are radically simple. Home is a secure place where one's needs, erotic and otherwise, can be licitly satisfied in accordance with the sacraments of the social and religious order. A hotel therefore suggests, not a resort—a place of pleasure and excitement—but a place of threatening disquiet, dominated by instincts that subvert the legal and familial orders. The study house and old Jerusalem, however, are the symbolic homes of the Holy Spirit—the dovelike, maternal presence which presides over all the stable, satisfying forms of existence.

There is an almost comic redundancy in the rendering of the motif here. The speaker's ordeal has the quality of a grotesque, silent-film animation; it synchronizes all the patterns of displacement and harassment accessible to Agnon's imagination. There is a touch of Chaplin in it, and of

Jacques Tati, but also of Saul Bellow's rooming-house heroes, of Hermann Broch's dwellers of cities under siege, and of Moon Mullins and his brethren of Sunday-paper habitat. The motif is a not unfamiliar Agnonic one: that the world is indeed a place of perpetual and meaningless motion, where it is impossible to come to rest because of obstacles to order, civility, decency, communication, and ordinary human life.

What we see of Berlin underscores such a concept of life. We enter a world in which everything has been sacrificed to the war machine. Natural foods, fibers, and fabrics are scarce; only synthetics are available. As in *A Guest for the Night,* moreover, amputees abound. And at the center of the tale stands the landlady's returning son, who, having lost his mind, has become a golem—a flesh-and-blood robot. Altogether, human relationships are denatured and fragmented. The narrator must report to the draft board regularly to see when he is to serve as cannon fodder. The city has become a mad anthill, with people scurrying to outsmart a torpid bureaucracy and to make shift in a regime where everyone has become an object of a disfunctional utility. People either emote histrionically or lack feeling altogether. They nurse their own griefs and grievances and have no sense of anyone else's. It seems no accident that the narrator's sculptor friend produces a studio full of distorted human shapes, and that several crucial scenes are set in a zoo, where a lion tamer called Peter Temper—one of the narrator's few communicants—is employed.

War is thematically vital to the story, but war only intensifies the modern condition. The deepest corruption is in the intimate sexual life, and it is clear that such corruption is no novelty. Again and again the narrator—a small-town Galician, who affirms the ancestral values—is horrified by what he sees. He is shocked when he hears that Aunt Clothilde, a bareback rider and his first pension keeper's sister-in-law, had become the owner of a riding school after her husband found her in bed with an aristocratic lover. He seems equally shocked by the fact that he is told this by one of Clothilde's nieces who obviously has designs on him.

He, too, is obviously both the subject and the object of lascivious desire. Hedwig Munkel, herself the bastard daughter of a rich old farmer, lolls provocatively in his room when she serves him breakfast. And he seems to have an affair with still another girl—Hildegarde, Clothilde's niece—and seems afflicted with further erotic imaginings.

Yet his response to the carrying-on around him is one of unabashed, unselfconscious dismay. He mouths wistful pieties about what the world is coming to and, like the Guest, laments the passing of the old *shtetl* virtues. Indeed, the decline of the ancestral culture bulks large in the novella. We hear of it in the course of the speaker's visits with one Dr. Mittel, a bibliographer who catalogues the truckloads of sacred books sent home as booty from the eastern front and mourns the fact that there is no one left to peruse them. And when we meet people who should be interested in the sacred texts, they turn out to be phony Galician pietists, assembled with a view to making a quick profit as middlemen in the sale of a dead scholar's library.

By referring to the old values, the narrator of "Thus Far" establishes a standard by which to judge both the city of sin and himself. For, with his niggling self-pity and his smug revulsion from the pain and the corruption of his surroundings, the protagonist of the novella is probably one of Agnon's most unpleasant characters. His self-involvement brings both the Guest and the speaker of "The Book of Deeds" to mind. Like them, he lacks the capacity for sympathy or charity, much as he lacks firm self-knowledge. And his judgments have a gross moralism which is the more grotesque because, according to the very standards he judges others by, he himself is often culpable.

In rendering him, Agnon seems to crystallize a growing sense of the speaker's repulsiveness. He does not, to be sure, undercut him in any blatant way. The character's discourse bumbles on in the flat, unmodulated cadence of all the other narrators of his type. In fact, his pieties are so similar (in form at least) to the pieties of the traditionalist tales that we may be led to lend him credence and to assume that Agnon sympathizes with him. But we know Agnon's devious relationship to his traditionalist modes. Even if we do not bring Agnon's own attitude to bear on him, however, the speaker of "Thus Far" seems both flat and stupid. He palls on us; we come to feel that he pays a terrible price for his seeming certainty. It is as if Agnon, though willing to use him to project his vision of modernity, must acknowledge his limits as an observer—and as a man.

The disquieting thing is that *Agnon's* sense of the world, as rendered here, seems to be as stale, flat, and mechanical as his protagonist's. We recognize in it elements of a familiar reality, perhaps of the world we know. We note the literary and philosophic sources from which the governing images are drawn. We may even concur in some of its judgments. But the final sense of truth called forth by a more richly imagined world and a more tightly wrought coherence eludes Agnon here. Neither the world that is rendered nor the subjectivity that renders it is vivid or commanding enough to justify the treatment given them.

Hence the sense of something derivative in the novella. So much of it derives from the repertory of expressionist art that it comes to have a dated, period quality. Only insofar as the imagery of Germany's social and moral collapse can serve as a touchstone to the universal condition does "Thus Far" stand as a telling statement on modernity. Within the bounds of that limitation, however, it seems to me that even its spread, its sprawl, and its incipient incoherence contribute to our sense of the modern world that is so central to Agnon's vision. Even the lack of fresh observation, which seems to mar it, contributes to the sense of a jaded world, without center, without hope, and without the possibility of valid transcendence.

[4]

Agnon's other late novellas project a far more integrated vision, and they do so in work of stunning beauty; together, they catch up all his major modernist themes. "Betrothed," "Ido and Enam," and "Forevermore" posit the deadness and dullness of the modern world.[8] They assume a universal condition of homelessness and a universal failure of communication. And they focus on the radical solitude of the individual, as well as on his utter incapacity to find satisfaction or fulfillment. In highly arcane, symbolic terms, they explore the effort to recapture the lost past and the way the submerged past surfaces to overwhelm the individual. Still more than *Yesteryear*, they intimate the psychological grounds of regression and collapse, even as they probe the part that reason, passion, and art can play in the life of the individual and the community.

"The Book of Deeds" and "Thus Far" present these themes diffusely, in terms that connote myopic incomprehension and bewilderment. In them, an individual who is cut off from both past and present is momentarily overwhelmed and has no real perspective on his experience. The late fables take a long view of such circumstances. Working with characters who choose (or rather seem to choose) their fate, Agnon examines their choice—of solitude, for example—and their striving. He not only evokes the quality of the modern world as he perceives it, but—within limits—contemplates some of its crucial aspects in a deliberate, distanced way.

All three fables center on quasi-Magian figures: on men who isolate themselves from common concerns in order to pursue esoteric knowledge of various sorts. In "Betrothed," Rechnitz seeks mysterious seaweed; in "Ido and Enam," Ginat investigates the secrets of a primordial civilization, perhaps of *the* primordial civilization; in "Forevermore," Adiel Amzeh pursues the secrets of Gumlidata, a Gothic city which fell to the Huns over a thousand years ago. What unites the three men is their choice of a priestlike seclusion and their dedication to a single pursuit. All three are overtaken by their fate as they strive to capture the objects of their quest.

In their self-sought seclusion they diverge radically from the victims of the other modernist work. These three are men with nearly heroic pretensions, who set themselves apart because of a passionate affinity for the object of their study. In a sense, they are the most active of Agnon's heroes. And their activity destroys them. In each case, however, it is suggested that such destruction is the condition for creation and that they somehow achieve a higher existence by yielding themselves to nullification.

Agnon's judgment of them stems in large part from his mistrust of the detached intellect. Rechnitz, we recall, turns out to be fixated first on his mother, then on his childhood girl friend; his scientific pursuits are a circuitous way back to the womb. No such reduction to a psychological motive is attempted in the treatment of Ginat—only a bold suggestion of the passion involved in the operation of the apparent intellectual detachment. Ginat, the great scientific ethnographer is destroyed when Gemulah, the instrument of his investigations, turns to him with a deadly passion. Presumably eliciting an equivalent passion in himself, she carries him to death.

Adiel Amzeh, on the other hand, is drawn into a total but compassionate relation to the object of his study. To pursue it, he must isolate himself in a leprosarium, where a priceless, pus-coated manuscript has survived since the fall of Gumlidata. In effect, Amzeh, the humanist scholar, who had been about to arrange for the publication of his studies by a philanthropic industrialist, must renounce the world in order to commune with the object of his interest. From being a detached observer of suffering he becomes an engaged and passionate sufferer—almost a leper himself.

The moral is transparent: cold rationality cannot put one in touch with the objects of knowledge; intellectual Eros is necessarily implicated by its objects in an extraintellectual way. Agnon suggests that his characters have no alternatives. They are coerced into their intellectual pursuits by something obscure within themselves and are swept to their doom by the tide of feeling into which their pursuits draw them.

For the vision of these fables looks beyond the merely modern world. Each of them suggests an opposition between a vain, dead, mechanical, violence-ridden world and an inner world that is full of magic and vitality, but also of danger. "Betrothed" and "Ido and Enam" directly involve their protagonists with a moonstruck woman, who is both the object of their sexual interest and a symbol of the feminine, passionate aspects of their souls. "Forevermore" involves Amzeh with no woman directly. But the chronicle of Gumlidata's fall—the text he has been seeking all his life, which completely engrosses him after he finds it—centers on a woman stranger, a Hun with a foster-sibling affinity for the birds and the beasts, who betrays the town to her people.

Agnon suggests that the objects of the most distant speculation, as of the most immediate passion, carry one into a realm of soul-consuming danger that completely takes possession of one, even when it does not openly destroy. Finally, there is in these tales a sense of adventure which the typical Agnonic protagonist can admire and—vicariously—enjoy. It is a realm of spiritual and passional experience, which lives in the imagination and is made up of intoxicating music, infinitely seductive women, and virile warriors, a realm which is both of the flesh and of the spirit and which cannot be embodied in the day-to-day life of any man.

Gemulah, the moonstruck girl (and neurasthenic wife) of "Ido and Enam," symbolizes the remotest reaches of the ancestral tradition. The three men who pursue her represent, as I have already suggested, various responses to the tradition. But she also symbolizes a dimension of the soul within each of the men and an aspect of life which eludes domestication or fixity of any sort. That aspect is feminine, musical, artistic, and beyond direct apprehension. Ordinary men, like the narrator of "Ido and Enam," can only catch snatches of her music through the words of the hymns that Ginat has transcribed.

And that music is the perpetual lure for men who seek a composure that lies above and beyond the incessant, meaningless movement of ordinary life. In the modern world, as Agnon presents it, the song beguiles those who seek it—though it finally enslaves or destroys them. It is implicit, however, everywhere and at all times. It troubles Dinah in "Agunot," and is probably crooned (even to the old rabbi) by the bereaved figure who symbolizes the Congregation of Israel, mourning her lost lover and craving union with him. For Eros, as Agnon conceives of it—in the ancestral world as much as in the modern—is restless and insatiable. Men, incomplete and aching, are consciously or unconsciously driven toward unions that might "complete" them. Instead, the pursuit itself destroys, since union itself is unattainable goal.

In the ancestral world, Eros seems to have a way of binding itself in forms and relationships that give it a certain stability. But even there it bursts the bounds of convention and comfort and seeks hopeless objects in hopeless ways. The difference between the ancestral world and the modern is that the pain, the violence, and the wrenching are not so great in the ancestral as in the modern world. The cause is presumably the ancestral mediation of the soul's longing by means of traditional forms and objects.

The parables suggest, however, that anyone who reaches

for the ultimate beauty or the ultimate truth, in any time, in any place, is subject to the dangers to which Ginat is exposed. Ginat and Gamzu are "modern" men, and their relation to Gemulah is fraught with modern perturbations. But their experience echoes the Talmudic parable, which tells of four rabbis who entered the orchard (*pardes,* or Paradise, but also an abbreviation of words referring to the modes of interpreting the Bible) of mystic truth, and of how "one emerged intact, one peered and was damaged (blinded), one dropped dead—and one hacked away at the roots of the plantings." Agnon does not depict four rabbis, and the truth Gemulah symbolizes is not the mystic lore of the rabbinic tradition. But the process seems to be analogous: a reaching for the ultimate object of ultimate desire, and a need for some special limits and regulations in relation to that object.

Indeed, from this point of view, the modern world in Agnon's work becomes, not a reflection of things-as-they-are-now, but a *symbol* of the mutable world, where men live in a condition of doubt and insecurity, striving to reach beyond its limits as best they can, even as they are lured by the siren song of their imaginations. "Ido and Enam" and "Forevermore"—and, to a lesser degree, "Betrothed"—evoke a sense of abstraction from common life in general as well as from the modern world in particular. There is the conviction in all three tales that both the life of the spirit and the life of the feelings are lived outside the light of common day. And that "outside" excludes not only the public world, but also the normative familial and erotic worlds, such as the bustling world of the Jaffa burghers in "Betrothed" and the restless world of homeless lovers in "Ido and Enam."

Hence the intense solitude around which the richly pop- ulated world of Agnon's more conventional work revolves: the solitude of the dreaming soul and the aspiring mind, be- yond contact and community with others. It is an awesome solitude, because it is unredeemable and because its relent- less demands cannot be lessened by knowledge of its rigors. But it is, in an ambivalent way, a tragic solitude, because all those who have the power and the vision to embrace it are open to the anguish (but also the ecstasy) experienced in contemplating it. What the late fables celebrate is the con- stancy of its pursuit and the chanciness of its apprehension; these works are concerned with naked, unalleviated con- templation of the highest objects of desire and informed by a tormenting awareness that such objects are not to be pos- sessed, since it is they who are always the possessors. The specifically Zionist and Judaic dimensions of "Ido and Enam" are oriented to only one facet of the larger circum- stance. It is a foregone conclusion, within that novella, that the spirit of old Israel, as embodied in Gemulah, cannot be domesticated in new Jerusalem.

In this aspect of its theme, "Ido and Enam" merely spells out what had been stated in *Yesteryear:* that the resurrec- tion of the ancestral civilization is an honorable compulsion but a hopeless pursuit. "Ido and Enam" extends the thesis by evoking, through Gemulah, some of the larger psychic horizons of the impulse to resurrect the lost Jerusalem, ren- dering them in a more tightly organized aesthetic pattern. But it also generalizes the motif by linking Gemulah to both the prehistorical world *and* to infantile experience. The suggestion is made that the striving forward in spirit and desire is always a going backward, and that its object is a union with the primordial which can be achieved only in death. Furthermore, the story intimates a process that is presumably at work in all of Agnon's defeated protagonists. Their essential passivity and laxness of will are rooted in a dependent yearning toward a union which, in its symbiotic essence, is tantamount to death.

Why this need be so is an open question. All of Agnon's major characters are subject to a passivity and a set of regressive yearnings that are easily explicable within the terms of the pattern explored in the late fables and *Yesteryear*. Obviously, the pattern figures wherever Agnon's imagination is deeply engaged. Yet it would not be sufficient to say that Agnon's imagination is haunted by such images of union and communion and the psychological patterns they form. The question remains: What significance, beyond a personal one, do they have? And to that question, it seems to me, Agnon's fiction offers no decisive answer. It only insists on the centrality of its preoccupations in both the ancestral scene and the modern world.

[8]
The Limits of
the Quest

Looking back over all of Agnon's work, there seems no doubt that *Yesteryear* clinches his emergent vision of the world, and not of the modern world alone. It carries his perception of the shape of modern Jewish history to its logical conclusion and, doing so, enunciates his sense of the void that underlies existence itself. Having read it, one recalls that the Yudel world, the world evoked so richly in *The Bridal Canopy, did* have existence—an existence that haunts *Yesteryear* too. But one is also provoked to contemplate the fact that Yudel's world constitutes, for Agnon, a retreat from the desolation of the present and a way of redeeming the deathliness of his own being: a deathliness that is at the core of *Yesteryear* and of Agnon's entire imaginative vision.

For *Yesteryear* confronts the limits, not only of the Zionist endeavor, but also of life and striving themselves, sounding all the motifs of the earlier work. The narrative voice strives to echo the grace notes of the traditionalist tales; Reb Alter echoes the all-embracing piety of the ancestral types. But here, at last—and far more than in *A Guest for the Night*—we see the futility of the effort. The narrative voice—Zionist rather than pietist, to be sure—is wholly fatuous when measured in terms of the realities it tells us about. So, implicitly, are the delicate *Liebestods* and the romantic fantasies of the ancestral tales on the one hand and *A Simple Story* on the other. Art itself is seen as a noble but futile effort. Blaukopf's paintings reflect the grim realities of his life, but they themselves are doomed: his wife, we are told, will leave his canvases to molder in the dank cellar where they lived.

Blaukopf's work, like Reb Alter's vision, ends up on the slag heap of history. Like the Enamite hymns recorded by Ginat in "Ido and Enam," the paintings depend on kindly accident for survival, and even when they manage to survive, they depend on the redeeming grace of an imagination that is by benign accident aware of their existence. Clearly, Agnon thinks in the same way of his own work, which is so assiduously dedicated to the evocation of the ancestral world and its survivals. Agnon's writings may allow us to glimpse the old ways, the old truth, and the old problems; they may attune us to the soul's longings and its vicissitudes as it lives within the husks of the flesh, in the present world. But his work has no power in the world and cannot ward off the sheer deathliness that informs both history and the self.

One is disposed, when contemplating Agnon's work in this light, to render its essential quality in terms of an old rabbinic legend. The midrash tells that when King David's time had come, the angel of death approached his palace. He could not accomplish his mission, however, because David, the Psalmist, was engrossed in singing the praises of the Lord. So long as David sang, he was invulnerable; only when he stopped, even if merely for a moment, could death touch him.

Agnon, one senses, has an analogous relation, not to God, but to his craft. His sensibility is pervaded by intimations of mortality, of the transcience of his own being and of all the things he values. His writing is a kind of whittling in the dark, to charm away the terror of the dark and of all that darkness signifies.

One might say that all art is such a charming: Shakespeare's sonnets are meant to outlast the brazen monuments of time, and Blake's Albion is that eternity of art which artists win in their struggle with time. I think there is a special quality in Agnon's effort, however. It is not only that his sense of mortality is compounded by his consciousness of the mortality of what he most values—that is, the ancestral traditions, to which he clings. It is, rather, that he makes his art out of his sense of his own mortality, so that he elaborates a vision in which history itself is rooted in a sense of loss.

The images that dominate Agnon's fiction are images of desolation, loss, and death. *Agunot*—bereaved souls—grope in the darkness of the world, seeking their lost mates; Menashe Haim gorges himself until he stinks and ends as a lonely mendicant, wandering on the roads of life; even Reb Yudel, with all the jolliness of his adventures, seems—as I have already noted—to be cherished partly for his blind movement over the roads and crossroads of Galicia. In the ancestral world, there are also Raphael the scribe, in the story that bears his name, embracing the shade of his dead mate; Gershom, in "The Outcast," sucking life from the dugs of thought, sighing out his soul in song; a lonely gravedigger, in an early lyric tale, necrophilically enamored of a once-glimpsed maiden; Ovadiah, the Maimed One, in the story of that name, who pays for his single moment of happiness with a stay in the hospital; and so on.

Outside the ancestral world, loss remains the salient theme. Hemdat has lost his grandfather's Way. Hershel has lost Blumah and the world of romance she stirred in his imagination. The Guest lives in a tenebrous realm, peopled with shadows of past lives and past worlds, and is haunted by the fact of pastness itself. Yitzhak dreams of his mother's hallowed kisses, and yearns ambivalently for Yudel and his ways. Above all, in *Yesteryear*, there is the overwhelming horror of the drought, of Balak, and of the terror induced by Balak, as well as by the sense that "the face of the generation is the face of a dog" and that the dogginess of this particular generation involves a pestilential murderousness from which there is no escape.

Nothing in all of Agnon's works has the force of Balak and the nihilism his treatment implies. It is as though, after much beating back of his central terrors, Agnon suddenly grasps them in one stupendous metaphor: Balak. And that metaphor is "set" in relation to the central Agnonic type and Agnonic problems in such a way that it illuminates the entire field of his vision. Yitzhak remains as ineffectual and ultimately as opaque as any of Agnon's other protagonists, but the implications of his world and experience are wholly crystallized. Those implications are relentless. Agnon's special achievement in *Yesteryear* lies in the confrontation of nullity and negation in their most extreme forms.

If one has any argument with Agnon—as I, in the last analysis, do—it springs from his failure to take hold of those implications sooner and to press them relentlessly to the end. Even the late parables, which do work in terms of the vision enunciated in *Yesteryear*, begin to sweeten its bitter pill of negation. Indeed, even *Yesteryear* is at times in danger of dulling its edge, owing to the sweet turnings of gentleness exemplified by its benign pietists and to the flatness of the Blaukopf characterization. Agnon has no real stomach for his harshest insights. Much as Yitzhak averts his eyes from the horror in himself, Agnon struggles to fill the void of his terror and unbelief with lovely evocations: even the doggy scavenger world of *Yesteryear* seems excessively ornamented—as, say, the horrors of *Titus Andronicus* are gilded, though in another way, with the honey of Shakespeare's mellifluous conceits.

To argue with a writer on these grounds—and especially a writer of Agnon's stature—is to argue dire issues. It is to say that, in the final accounting, Agnon sidesteps the harshest and most meaningful confrontations of all. But it is also to acknowledge, even as one points to his failure, that only his courage and his boldness allow us to perceive the problem at all. Only because Agnon's genius gives his innermost life so rich an objectification, are we able to question its integrality at all. His genius takes the essential passivity of a protagonist who is clearly congenial to his imagination and makes it the basis of a series of historical investigations so rigorous that we can say they are not rigorous enough. It is Agnon's genius that points to the abysmal quality of existence in ways that provoke us to say that he has refused to fathom its depths.

Agnon's gift is such that it provokes the highest expectations and impels us to make the most aggressive demands. The pleasures the work affords compensate for many limitations: the terrible muting of his peoples' passions, whether they be of love or of rage; the chilling lack of sympathy with ordinary human aspiration; the tamping of dramatic urgencies; and the cloying indulgence of sheer verbal effect. These limitations often yield in the face of the sheer beauty of Agnon's evocations and of his astonishing architectonic virtuosity in the projection of themes and of worlds. More than anything, they yield, for those who have the patience to follow the development of the entire body of his work, in terms of the larger architecture of the revelation that is apparent in the context of the whole: an architecture that indeed has "epic" dimensions, and that embraces so much that is vital to the history of his culture over hundreds of years. The awareness of Agnon's strengths, however, is somehow again subordinated to the intuition that something essential is missing: the agony of final confrontation, which will bring muscle and bone and blood and guts into the wrestling with the angel of nullity—not so much sweet singing and exquisite purling of song.

A Bibliographical Note
on Agnon's Published Work

Agnon's fiction has been collected in two comprehensive editions, both called *Kol kitve Shmuel Yosef 'Agnon* (The Complete Works of Shmuel Yosef Agnon). The first (which I shall refer to as the first *Works*) was inaugurated by Schocken Verlag in Berlin in 1931. It grew, first in Berlin and then in Tel Aviv, as Agnon released new works. The last volume of this edition appeared in Tel Aviv in 1952. The second comprehensive edition (which I shall refer to as the second *Works*) was published by Schocken in Tel Aviv, in seven volumes, in 1953; an eighth volume was added in 1962. The volumes of these editions are as follows:

First *Complete Works of Shmuel Yosef Agnon* (11 vols.; Berlin and Tel Aviv: Schocken, 1931–1952)

I–II. *Hakhnassat kala* [The Bridal Canopy]. Berlin, 1931. First publication of this novel.

III. *Me'az ume'ata* [From Then and from Now]. Berlin, 1931. Stories, traditional and modern.

IV. *Sipure ahavim* [Love Stories]. Berlin, 1931.

V. *Sipur pashut* [A Simple Story]. Berlin, 1935. First publication of this novel.

VI. *Beshuva vanahat* [Slow and Steady]. Berlin, 1935. Mainly tales of the ancestral world.

VII. *Oreah nata lalun* [A Guest for the Night]. Tel Aviv, 1939. First publication of this novel.

VIII. *'Elu ve'elu* [Of Such and of Such]. Tel Aviv, 1941. Stories, ancestral and modern.

IX. *Temol shilshom* [Yesteryear]. Tel Aviv, 1945. First publication of this novel.

X. *Samukh venir'e* [Near and Apparent]. Tel Aviv, 1951. Stories.

XI. *'Ad hena* [Thus Far]. Tel Aviv, 1952. Stories.

Second *Complete Works of Shmuel Yosef Agnon* (8 vols.; Tel Aviv: Schocken, 1953–1962)

I. *Hakhnassat kala* [The Bridal Canopy]. Tel Aviv, 1953.

II. *'Elu ve'elu* [Of Such and of Such]. Tel Aviv, 1953. Stories, ancestral and modern.

III. *'Al kapot haman'ul* [Upon the Handles of the Lock]. Tel Aviv, 1953. Love stories, including "A Simple Story."

IV. *Oreah nata lalun* [A Guest for the Night]. Tel Aviv, 1953.

V. *Temol shilshom* [Yesteryear]. Tel Aviv, 1953.

VI. *Samukh venir'e* [Near and Apparent]. Tel Aviv, 1953. Stories.

VII. *'Ad hena* [Thus Far]. Tel Aviv, 1953. Stories.

VIII. *Ha'esh veha'etsim* [The Fire and the Trees]. Tel Aviv, 1963. Ancestral stories.

The problems of Agnon's bibliography are formidable. He has published in many places and in many formats, and he is an inveterate reviser. The most comprehensive bibliographic account appears in Arnold Band's *Nostalgia and Nightmare* (Berkeley and Los Angeles: University of California Press, 1968).

Translations

Agnon's major works are increasingly accessible in European languages. Schocken Books in New York has issued English translations: *In the Heart of the Seas*, translated by I. M. Lask (1948); *The Bridal Canopy*, translated by I. M. Lask (1967);

A Guest for the Night, translated by Misha Louvish (1968); and *Two Tales*, translated by Walter Lever ("Betrothed" and "Ido and Enam," 1966). Schocken will publish a volume of stories in 1970, and a translation of *A Simple Story* is being prepared.

For readers of German, it should be noted that the German translations are generally judged to be better than the English ones. *Nur wie ein Gast zur Nacht* (A Guest for the Night), translated by Karl Steinschneider, was published in Frankfort by S. Fischer in 1964; *Eine einfache Erzählung* (A Simple Story), translated by Karl Steinschneider, in Frankfort by S. Fischer in 1968; *Im Herzen der Meere und andere Erzählungen* ("In the Heart of the Seas" and Other Stories), translated by Karl Steinschneider and Max Strauss, in Zurich by Manessa Verlag in 1966; *Der Treuschwur* (Betrothed), translated by Tobias Rübner, in Frankfort by S. Fischer in 1966; and *Der Verstossene* (The Outcast), translated by N. N. Glatzer and Morris Spitzer, in Frankfort by Insel Verlag in 1964.

Contes de Jérusalem (Tales of Jerusalem), which includes French translations of the late fables, "A Whole Loaf," and the Balak segments of *Yesteryear*, was published in Paris by A. Michel in 1959, in a translation by R. and G. Casaril. *Racconti di Gerusalemme* (Tales of Jerusalem), containing the same material in Italian, was published in Verona by A. Mondadori in 1964, in a translation by E. M. Ottolenghi. The Spanish *En el corazón de los mares; y Lo torcida se endreza; El alejado* (In the Heart of the Seas; The Crooked Made Straight; The Outcast), translated by Angel Sabrido and Martin Ezcurdia, was published in Barcelona by Plaza and Janes in 1967. The Swedish *Trohetseden; berättelse* (Betrothed) and *Den Bortdrivne* (The Outcast), translated by Viveca Heyman, were published in Stockholm by A. Bonniers in 1967 and 1968, respectively.

Notes

Chapter 1. Agnon's Quest: An Overview

1. Baruch Kurzweil, in *Masot 'al sipure Shai 'Agnon* (Ramat Gan, 1963), states the case for viewing Agnon as an epic writer. Kurzweil is a passionate and an ideological reader, with axes to grind. But he is one of Agnon's most assiduous readers—and often one of his most astute partisans. E. M. Lipschütz, in *Shai 'Agnon* (Berlin, 1926), which is reprinted in *Ketavim*, II (1953), attempted to demonstrate that even Agnon's early traditionalist work was epic in conception. Altogether, Lipschütz' essay is both elegant and perspicuous.

2. Agnon's lyricism was evident very early. Y. H. Brenner spoke of it—and of its dangers—in 1913. See *Kol Kitve Y. H. Brenner* (Tel Aviv, 1960), pp. 319–320. Arnold Band, in *Nostalgia and Nightmare* (Berkeley, Calif., 1968), pegs Agnon as a neoromantic and, insofar as he pursues this thesis, implies that there is a lyric center in his work. Band's book is the most extensive on Agnon in any language. It has the most complete bibliography available and is useful in summing up the complexities of Agnon's development. It can also be of use in taking hold of particular works, offering as it does exhaustive structural and thematic analyses of everything of any note. Though it often loses the forest for the trees, it remains the best aid to the reader of English.

3. The most trenchant statement of the impulse toward

transcendence in Agnon's work, to my knowledge, is in Gavriel Moked, *Shivhe 'Adiel 'Amze* (Tel Aviv, 1957). Adi Zemach deals with it in *Hasifrut*, I (1968), 378–385.

4. Both "'Ido ve'Enam" ("Ido and Enam") and "Shevu'at 'emunim" ("Betrothed") appear in Vol. XI of the first *Works* and in Vol. VII of the second. Both appear in English in *Two Tales* (New York, 1966).

5. One of the extraordinary things about "Betrothed" is how it manages to suggest (to some readers at least) a complete Freudian and a complete Jungian view of Jacob's circumstance. It elaborates these by means of a set of religious and historical tropes, as well as by an action involving the clash of fate and free will, of Hebrews and Hellenes, and the like. Dov Sadan, in one of the most cunning pieces of close reading I know, anatomizes these dimensions of the tale (see " 'Agadat shiv'ah veshev'a," in *'Al Shai 'Agnon* [Tel Aviv, 1967]). Sadan is another of Agnon's incisive readers. His placement of Agnon in the annals of Hebrew literature and its attitude to the Jewish past ("'Arba'ah kerachim," *ibid.*) remains the most astute there is.

6. Kurzweil reads "Ido and Enam" interestingly (*Masot*, pp. 141–160). So do Meshulam Tochner ("'Al 'Ido ve'Enam," Ha'aretz, Oct. 3, 10, 1958) and Lea Goldberg ("'Agnon bishlosha kolot," *'Al Hamishmar*, Oct. 27, 1950).

7. Band, in the first chapter of *Nostalgia and Nightmare*, provides a convenient summary of essential information on Agnon's life and background.

8. "Agunot" is in Vol. III, pp. 233–251, of the first *Works*, and in Vol. 11, pp. 405–416, of his second.

9. *The Bridal Canopy* is available in English in a translation by I. M. Lask (New York, 1967). *Hakhnassat kala* first appeared as Vols. I and II of the first *Works*. It was reissued in 1953, in a heavily augmented version, as Vol. I of the second *Works*.

10. The original Hebrew edition of *Sipur pashut* appeared in 1935, as Vol. V of the first *Works*. It is in Vol. III (*'Al kapot haman'ul*) of the second *Works*. There is a German translation: *Eine einfache Erzählung*, trans. Karl Steinschneider (Frankfort, 1968).

11. The original Hebrew version of *Oreaḥ nata lalun* appeared in 1939 as Vol. VII of the first *Works*. It is Vol. IV of the second. The English translation appeared in New York in 1968, the German in Frankfort in 1964.

12. *Temol shilshom* appeared in 1945 as Vol. IX of the first *Works*, in 1953 as Vol. V. of the second.

13. The Chaplin link is an important one. It suggests numerous affinities. Sadan points it out.

14. Gershom Scholem points out the conservative classicist impulse that informs Agnon's style. See his, "Reflections on S. Y. Agnon," *Commentary*, XLIV (Dec. 1967).

15. It is one of the curious facts about the critical response to Agnon that few writers have recorded their negative answer to this question. There has been some ideological flak—at least there was, before the Holocaust—with regard to sentimentality and aestheticism. But for a good while now there has been no serious effort to come to grips with the limits of Agnon's achievement.

Chapter 2. The Whole Loaf: Agnon's Tales of the Ancestral World

1. The traditionalist work, reflecting the ancestral world, is for the most part in Vol. I (*Hakhnassat kala, The Bridal Canopy*, a novel); Vol. II (*'Elu ve'elu*, a collection of novellas, short stories, and folk tales); and Vol. VIII (*Ha'esh veha'etsim*, a collection of late short stories) of the second *Works*. I do not deal with *Ha'esh veha'etzim*.

2. The affirmative bias in Agnon's treatment of the *shtetl* is examined in Dov Sadan's excellent *'Al 'arba'at kerachav harishonim*, in his *'Al Shai 'Agnon* (Tel Aviv, 1967). Meshulam Tochner, in a variety of essays, defines the same phenomenon.

3. First *Works*, III, 234 ff. For bibliographic details see Chapter 1, n. 8, above. "Agunot" has undergone many revisions. I translate from the text of Vol. III (*Me'az ume'ata*, 1931) of the first *Works*. This is the text I use for all the passages I translate in this chapter. Agnon's process of revision is complicated and repays study. For the purpose of this study, whose emphasis is essentially developmental and historical, the first authoritative text seems the most revealing. My translation of "Agunot," from which the quotation in this section is taken, first appeared in *Congress Bi-Weekly*, XXXIII (Nov. 7, 1966), 21–26.

4. The interweaving of analogous actions, with the "splitting" of characters, is a fundamental technique of Agnon's fiction, traditionalist and modern. Gershon Shaked anatomized the technique in "Ba'ayot mivniot bitsirato shel Shai 'Agnon," in *Le'Agnon Shai*, ed. Sadan and Ephraim Urbach (Jerusalem, 1959), pp. 307–330. "Agunot" and "The Crooked Made Straight" are among the tales analyzed there (see pp. 319–322).

5. "Vehaya he'akov lemishor" is in Vol. III of the first *Works*, pp. 75–159. It is available in German in *Im Herzen der Meere und Andere Erzählungen*, trans. Karl Steinschneider and Max Strauss (Zurich, 1966).

6. First *Works*, III, 75.

7. *Ibid.*, p. 71.

8. "Agadat hasofer" is in Vol. III of the first *Works*, pp. 227–244.

9. *Ibid.*, p. 227.

10. *Ibid.*, p. 234.

11. "Hanidaḥ" is in Vol. III of the first *Works*, pp. 9–69.

12. *Ibid.*, p. 66.

13. *Ibid.*, p. 67.

14. *Ibid.*, p. 67.

15. *Ibid.*, pp. 68–69.

16. Vol. VI of the second *Works*.

17. Sadan, in the essays in the first section of *'Al Shai 'Agnon* (1967), deals most effectively with Agnon's sense of the grandeur of the past as compared to his own inadequacy in the present. Moked also touches on the theme.

Chapter 3. *The Bridal Canopy* and the Comedy of Providence

1. My discussion of *Hakhnassat kala* (*The Bridal Canopy*) is based on the 1931 text (first *Works*, Vols. I and II). I use this text because it embodies Agnon's initial conception. Translations of passages are my own, and are based on the 1931 text. The standard English translation is by I. M. Lask (New York, 1966).

2. Arnold Band stresses the ironic and parodic elements of the novel. His detailed analysis is to be found in *Nostalgia and Nightmare*, pp. 137 ff.

3. First *Works*, I, 9 (3). In citations of *The Bridal Canopy*, page references in parentheses are to the Lask translation.

4. *Ibid.*, pp. 9–10 (3).

5. First *Works*, II, 42 (288).

6. *Ibid.*, p. 43 (288).

7. *Ibid.*, p. 44 (289).

8. *Ibid.*, p. 45 (290).

9. *Ibid.*, p. 219 (373).

10. *Ibid.*, pp. 175–217. "The Song of the Alphabet" is

omitted from the Lask translation. It is mentioned, though, on p. 372. "The Song" is not only thematically central, but it is also crucial to the rhythm of the novel. It bridges the distance between the wedding feast and the final happy ending: an ending happier than anything even implied by the initial narrative resolution, with its hidden treasure, its reassembling of people met along the way, and the like.

11. *Ibid.*, pp. 93–94 (318–319).

12. *Ibid.*, p. 86 (not included in Lask).

13. The stories in "The Book of Deeds" were published between 1931 and 1951, when all twenty of them were finally gathered under that title in Vol. X of the first *Works*, which is Vol. VI of the second *Works*. The first collection, consisting of the five earliest tales, appeared in 1932.

14. "Lelot," (Vol. III, second *Works*) first appeared in Jaffa in 1913; "Giv'at hahol" (*ibid.*) was first published under the title "Tishre," in 1911.

15. Lea Goldberg analyzes the quality of Agnon's irony in "Shai 'Agnon, hasofer vegiboro," in *Le'Agnon* Shai, ed. Sadan and Urbach, pp. 47–62.

Chapter 4. Backwater, Buczacz: The World of Agnon's Youth

1. "Bin'arenu uvizkenenu" ("Young and Old Together") first appeared in Warsaw in 1923. It is included in Vol. IV of the first *Works* and in Vol. III of the second *Works*. *Sipur pashut* (*A Simple Story*) first appeared as Vol. V of the first *Works*, and is collected with other love stories in Vol. III of the second *Works*. I cite, for both stories, the text of Vol. III of the second *Works*. Neither story has been translated into English.

2. A. J. Brawer discusses the immediate social and political backgrounds of "Young and Old Together" in "Bin'arenu uvizkenenu bemisgeret haye mehabro," in *Yuval Shai*, ed. Kurzweil, pp. 39–48. Sadan sketches the prevailing spiritual ambience in " 'Al arb'aah krachim," in *'Al Shai 'Agnon*.

3. Second *Works*, III, 273.

4. *Ibid.*, p. 350.

5. *Ibid.*, p. 350.

6. *Ibid.*, p. 329.

7. The marvelous play of conflicting elements in *A Simple Story* is analyzed by Gershon Shaked in "Bat hamelech use'udat ha'em," in *Gazit*, XXIV, 135–147.

8. Second *Works*, III, 233.

9. *Ibid.*, p. 140.

10. *Ibid.*, p. 268.

11. *Ibid.*, pp. 271–272.

12. *Ibid.*, p. 91.

13. "Bidmi yameha" ("In the Flower of Her Youth," 1921), in Vol. IV of the first *Works* and Vol. III of the second *Works*, is the third of the more or less major works in which Agnon confronts the world of his youth. It is one of Agnon's more effective love stories, involving a marriage between a young woman and her mother's rejected lover, a Hebrew teacher who has returned from Vienna to the *shtetl* and devotes himself to deciphering graveyard inscriptions and writing the history of their town. In it, Akaviah Mazal and Tirzah "repair the flaw" in her mother's life. The mother has rejected Akaviah because of his poverty; Tirzah sets things straight by marrying him. Together, they achieve what seems to be happiness by withdrawing wholly from the public world of the present.

14. Again, one thinks here of the modes of romantic irony and its function in sustaining ambiguity and projecting ambiva-

lence. Again, see Lea Goldberg, "Shai 'Agnon, hasofer vegiboro," in *Le 'Agnon Shai*, ed. Sadan and Urbach.

Chapter 5. Between the Then and the Now: *A Guest for the Night*

1. *Oreaḥ nata lalun* appeared in 1939 as Vol. VII of the first *Works;* it is Vol. IV of the second. An English translation, *A Guest for the Night*, by Misha Louvish, appeared in New York in 1968, and a German translation by Karl Steinschneider in Frankfort in 1964. My quotations are from the Louvish translation. The most sensitive assessment of its literary and human values is in Simon Halkin's "Al Oreaḥ nata lalum," in *Le 'Agnon Shai*, ed. Sadan and Urbach.

2. *A Guest for the Night*, p. 2.

3. *Ibid.*, p. 5.

4. *Ibid.*, p. 2; italics mine.

5. *Ibid.*, p. 5; italics mine.

6. See Kurzweil, *Masot,* on "The Motif of the Late Return, . . ." (ch. xviii), for analysis of the recurrent theme of family, woman, house—and lockout.

7. *A Guest*, p. 111.

8. Gershom Shaked effectively analyzes the problematics of the Guest in "Hamesaper kisofer," in *Hasifrut*, I, 17–35.

9. *A Guest*, p. 165.

Chapter 6. Between the Now and the Then: *Yesteryear*

1. *Temol shilshom* appeared in 1945 as Vol. IX of the first *Works*, and in 1953 as Vol. V of the second. All the quotations from *Yesteryear* are in my translation. Page references are to

Vol. IX of the first *Works*.

  2. First *Works*, IX, 7.

  3. *Ibid.*

  4. *Ibid.*, p. 604.

  5. *Ibid.*, p. 441.

  6. *Ibid.*, p. 606.

  7. *Ibid.*, p. 607.

  8. *Ibid.*, p. 607.

Chapter 7. "The Whole Loaf": Tales of the Modern World

  1. Hemdat appears in the Jaffa setting in such tales as "Lelot" and "Giv'at Haḥol." A character called Hemdat, we recall, is also the speaker in "Young and Old Together."

  2. Five stories appeared under the title "Sefer Hama'asim" ("The Book of Deeds") in 1932, seven in 1939, thirteen in 1941, and the twenty that make up the final collection in 1951, in Vol. X of the first *Works*. "Sefer Hama'asim" is in Vol. VI of the second *Works*.

  3. "Pat shelema" first appeared in 1933. It is included in Vols. VIII (1941) and X (1951) of the first *Works*, and in Vol. VI of the second.

  4. *Masot*, pp. 86–94.

  5. *Nostalgia and Nightmare*, 189 ff.

  6. " 'Ad hena" appears in Vol. IX of the first *Works* and in Vol. VII of the second.

  7. Second *Works*, VII, 170.

  8. For bibliographical information on "Betrothed" and "Ido and Enam," see Chapter 1, note 4, above. " 'Ad 'Olam" first appeared in *Ha'arets* in 1954, and is included in Vol. VIII of the second *Works*. An English translation, with the title "For-

evermore," is included in *Israeli Stories*, ed. Joel Blocker (New York, 1962). All three tales appear in French in *Contes de Jérusalem* (Paris, 1959), and in Italian in *Racconti di Gerusalemme* (Verona, 1964). A German version of "Forevermore" appears in *Im Herzen der Meere und andere Erzählungen* (Zurich, 1966).

Index

205